MIND OVER MONEY

JOHN MALHAM BRIDGES

Scripture Union
130 City Road, London EC1V 2NJ

Credits Guy and Company (independent investment and pension consultants: 3 West Terrace, Eastbourne, East Sussex, BN21 4QX, tel 0323 22565) commented helpfully on the text, as did the staff of Credit Action (part of the Jubilee Centre, 3 Hooper Street, Cambridge CB1 2NZ, tel 0223 324034).

First published 1993

ISBN 0 86201 792 0

British Library Cataloguing-in-Publication Data. A catalogue record for this book is available from the British Library.

Cover design by Phil Thomson with illustration by Claire Davies.
Book design by Julian Smith with cartoons by Pantelis Palios.

Phototypeset by The Electronic Book Factory, Fife, Scotland. Printed and bound in Great Britain by Cox and Wyman Ltd, Reading, Berkshire.

CONTENTS

INTRODUCTION

This book is about money, literally the blood of our society. It is important to us because God says it is important to him. In the Bible God describes how Israel should behave in practical financial matters. Our society is a technologically different but materialistic consumer society too. Behind God's instructions were his own unchanging principles which apply to all human societies, including ours today. This book seeks to describe those principles in relation to modern financial realities.

Personal circumstance and taste give many answers to essentially similar problems. The fixed point is God's word since human customs, law and markets change constantly. If we were to cover every permutation we would need a book as long as the Bible. I have tried instead to give a sight of the ground over which one travels when planning finances. If you know who to question, what to ask, and how to interpret the answers your decisions can reflect God's word and the facts concerning the situation. In our faith there are few rigid rules. We live by grace, not law. Our challenge is to discover how God wishes us to apply his guiding principles to ourselves.

We also play in teams. The final chapter is a vision for what might be if Christians work together financially. The vision is mine and some will hate its specifics. Its aim is only to spark ideas and action (the two 'networks' have yet to be proven and I'd love to develop the ideas with people with burdens for evangelism or fair trade issues). What is your vision? If we all 'think big and think dangerously' Satan will hate it.

Chapter One

WHAT THE BIBLE SAYS ABOUT MONEY

'What's it looking like this week, Jim?' Robert Ward, pastor of St Allsbright Church, Buttemuddled-in-the-Weye, carefully manoeuvred two large mugs of tea round the church office door and closed it behind him with his foot.

Jim Philips was one of Robert's co-leaders. He had just finished counting the offering from that morning's service. 'Forty-one pounds and thirteen pence. Plus the covenanted giving makes this week's total five-hundred and forty-odd pounds.'

Robert put a mug on the desk at which Jim was seated, then settled into the armchair that he used, among other things, for meditating on problems. He sipped his tea and prayed quietly for a few moments. This was the time to share a conviction that had been growing in his mind since Christmas.

'Jim, I think I should teach this flock about money.'

Jim had a great deal of respect for Robert's skill as a pastor and teacher. He had worked hard to get him as vicar some years earlier and had supported him loyally in fights with the parish hierarchy ever since. With forty-six years in the parish himself, however, he also felt well qualified to advise Robert on the wisdom of certain bright ideas.

'Be careful. Look what happened when you did that series on sex last year.'

'One of the best attended series of sermons ever.' Robert briefly savoured the memory of the storm he had generated. 'We made some good contacts among the youngsters. Church was relevant to them for once. And hopefully it'll reduce the number of sexual welfare problems I'll have to deal with in future years.'

'It was precisely its relevance to them that got Mrs Pomfrey so upset. She doesn't come to church because it's relevant, she comes to get away from real life!'

'But the Christian faith is real life,' retorted Robert. 'Life doesn't get more real, does it?'

'Robert, I'm just reminding you that most people at St Allsbright don't know much about actually *living* the Christian faith. Heck, most of them wouldn't recognize Jesus if he turned up for Sunday service,' Jim chuckled at the irony, 'and if they knew him they probably wouldn't want him as a member of this church!'

'Too much of a troublemaker,' agreed Robert with a smile. 'It's comforting to know our Lord also had such problems. But a preacher's job is still to comfort the disturbed and disturb the comfortable.'

'I can certainly see you doing that! Why the sudden concern with money?'

'It's far from sudden, believe me. We had about two hundred people in church this morning. At least sixty per cent are salaried. Suppose the average income is only ten thousand a year. That means we have a congregation with pretax earnings of over a million a year. Under Mosaic law we'd be contributing about two thousand a week to the church's work. We hardly give a quarter of that!'

'We don't live under Mosaic law, either! We're saved by grace, don't forget.'

'Agreed. But does the fact that we live under a better covenant mean we should give less?' Robert warmed to his subject. 'I recall Jesus saying something about honesty, too. Some of those ten thousand a year incomes support six-bedroom houses with swimming pools, timeshares, a brace of Mercs, and holidays in Bali and the Seychelles every six months.

'Ugh! It's one of those New Age travellers.'

Either we're witnessing miracles, or someone's hired the type of accountant who can make two and two equal any number they think of.'

'What have you got in mind? Some people will get really upset if you suggest that God has a claim on their money, or that ripping off the taxman's un-Christian. They'll salve their consciences by convincing themselves that you're doing it to line your own pocket. After all, most of them think they're doing the church a favour simply by turning up. You start preaching Christ crucified and biblical standards of stewardship and they may all leave.'

Robert took another swig of tea. 'You're forgetting the Holy Spirit. This is one of those occasions when I think we must tell the truth and face the consequences. As to how? Well, being saved by God's grace, not by our own efforts, I think the best approach is to bring out the principles within the Bible's teaching on money and let the Holy Spirit show each individual how to apply them in their own lives. Did you know that money is actually one of the most talked-about subjects in the Bible? That implies it's one of God's favourite topics. I'd hardly be doing my job properly if I ignored it, would I?'

A couple of hours exploring Scripture the next morning yielded a prodigious amount of raw material. He sorted it into a number of sections and picked out the major themes. He knew that if he tried to cover every aspect in minute detail he risked being irrelevant to many of his listeners. That confirmed his instinct to stick to basic principles in the talks and leave it to each individual to determine their detailed responses.

It was rare for anyone to take notes during sermons, even the committed, so Robert decided to write a study guide for each of the two talks. Whether he would need to do any follow-up would depend on the reaction. His present sermon series had only four more Sundays to run, by which time it would be mid-March: a perfect time for a series on money, just when the tax returns arrived and the accountants started to earn their corn! And so Robert wrote . . .

'ALL THINGS COME FROM YOU, O LORD . . .'

'Love of money is the root of all evil': one of the least understood and most misquoted phrases in the Bible. A whole mythology has grown up around it. Some Christians act as if money itself is evil. Others feel that it is merely an unsavoury fact of life. To judge from the amount of the Bible devoted to it though, money is a subject of great importance to God.

This study guide aims to draw out the principles that lie within the Bible's references to money. Although the writings themselves were for people living in a different society, they are underpinned by certain principles which reflect God's unchanging nature and apply in any society, including our own. We can, with the Holy Spirit's guidance, apply them to our own lives in our present cultural and economic circumstances.

The guidance of the Holy Spirit is vital. God's people are no longer bound in slavish obedience to Old Testament rules. Paul wrote to the Romans: 'Christ is the end of the law so that there may be righteousness for everyone who believes' (Romans 10:4). Because Christ died on the cross for our rebellion against God, the price of our disobedience has already been paid. Isaiah sums it up when he says of Christ: '. . . he was crushed for our iniquities; the punishment that brought us peace [ie the end of our war with God] was upon him and by his wounds we are healed' (Isaiah 53:5). We cannot earn God's salvation by obeying his laws. Paul makes that clear: 'I do not set aside the grace of God, for if righteousness could be gained through the law, Christ died for nothing' (Galatians 2:21). To the Galatians he wrote: 'But if you are led by the Spirit, you are not under law' (Galatians 5:18). God's law is now to be 'written on our hearts, . . . no longer on tablets of stone' (2 Corinthians 3:2–3). Part of our daily living in Christ is the process of being reshaped by God's Spirit so that pleasing him is not a matter of an external code but becomes an inner dynamic. That process includes seeking his will for the resources he has given us, including wealth.

Money is a good thing

There is a considerable amount of Scripture devoted to money: laws governing its use, histories of peoples' success and failure with it and the consequences of both. In addition there is the teaching of Jesus and the apostles which applies God's changeless principles to believers living under God's new covenant.

In the New Testament John describes heavenly beings singing that the Lamb (Jesus) is worthy to receive 'power and wealth and wisdom and strength and honour and glory and praise' (Revelation 5:12). All the things described can be used well, or Jesus would not want to receive them. He would certainly not be worthy of receiving something evil. It is clear, then, that wealth can be good.

Through the prophet Haggai, God makes clear that all wealth is his own. 'The silver is mine and the gold is mine, declares the Lord,' he told Israel (Haggai 2:8). At that time Israel had been working very hard to accumulate wealth, individually and nationally, much as we are today. In chapter one the Lord points out that he had been allowing them to 'earn wages, only to put them in a purse with holes in it' (Haggai 1:5–6). They had forgotten that God had promised they would always be his 'treasured possession' (Exodus 19:5) and were concentrating on getting material wealth. Despite their efforts, though, wealth was slipping away as fast as they could make it. God continues: 'Why? Because of my house, which remains a ruin, while each of you is busy with his own house' (Haggai 1:9). Only when the people turned from their own priorities (material wealth in this case) and worked according to God's did they receive his blessings (Haggai 2:15–19). Money is an important resource owned by God. It is given to us to be used in accordance with his will and God has a record of thwarting those who adopt other priorities.

Serving God or Mammon

In the Sermon on the Mount Jesus teaches: 'Do not store up for yourselves treasures on earth . . . but . . . in heaven . . . For where your treasure is, there will your heart be also'

(Matthew 6:19–21). He is describing two kinds of wealth: spiritual wealth, an everlasting commodity; and economic wealth, which is transitory. Jesus, a master of clarity, makes a simple point: the objects you treasure will be those you worship. In this case the choice is between spiritual treasures, stored up by doing God's will, and economic treasures.

The writer of Hebrews uses Moses to illustrate this choice in action: 'By faith Moses . . . refused to be known as the son of Pharaoh's daughter. He chose to be mistreated along with the people of God rather than to enjoy the pleasures of sin [meaning self and self-interest] for a short time' (Hebrews 11:24–25). Moses decided to give up Egypt. He gave up a comfortable lifestyle, public worship of himself, abundant power and fantastic wealth. He followed God instead, spending many years tramping round deserts with a bunch of grumbling malcontents. Can you imagine how career-minded, status-conscious twentieth century parents would have reacted if he'd been their son? Moses could have told God that he preferred economic security. Fortunately for the slaves in Egypt he followed God's plan rather than his own.

No one, taught Jesus, can serve two masters. God and Mammon are both potentially masters of our lives. Mammon is often translated as 'money', although it is better used of a spiritual force that controls people through money. It is part of that spiritual entity 'the world', perhaps best defined as all who reject God's rule in the person of Jesus. Some of the symptoms of serving Mammon are illustrated in the story of the rich young ruler (Matthew 19:16–24; Mark 10:17–24; Luke 18:18–24).

In Jesus' culture, 'service' meant slavery. While there is nothing actually wrong in possessing considerable material wealth, someone who measures life's fulfilment in, for example, consumer durables is probably a slave to them. They have become his god. If asked which religion he follows, he ought to reply 'Materialism', since he has placed his faith in material possessions. He would be in severe difficulties if God asked him to give them up. The rich young ruler was a wealthy man from a respectable household, a pillar of the community, no doubt. Yet he was asked to give up all he had to follow

Jesus. Luke records, 'he became very sad, because he was a man of great wealth.' Looking with compassion at the young man, torn between two masters, God and Mammon, Jesus observed: 'How hard it is for the rich to enter the kingdom of God!' The rich ruler was so addicted to his wealth and status in the world that he had become enslaved and couldn't live without them: a wealth junkie!

Let us not be too hard on the rich man. How many of us might find ourselves torn between two masters if the Lord asked us to give up our present status and ambitions to serve soup to the homeless, for instance? The lives of a number of missionaries reveal similar conflicts over their callings. What would our family and friends think? Would we care what they said? What we do with our money is a test of our love for God. How much of it is devoted to his work, how much of it to our own gratification? How much serves 'the world', how much the Kingdom?

In the parable of the talents (Luke 19:11–27) Jesus teaches us that God, who entrusts us with wealth, will expect accounts. How faithful will our trusteeship appear? God expects from today's believers the same as he demanded from Israel in Haggai's day. The 'good and faithful servants' were those who went and invested what they had been given to produce greater returns for their master. The one who buried his talent and failed to use it as his master intended, lost it. 'Whoever can be trusted with very little can also be trusted with much . . . So if you have not been trustworthy in handling worldly wealth, who will trust you with true riches?' (Luke 16:10–12). It is the good stewards of the Lord's resources on this earth who will be the ones blessed with everlasting spiritual wealth.

Along with the advice the Bible is also encouraging. Jacob lived a life marked by periods of faithfulness to God interspersed with flagrant disobedience. While destitute and a refugee, fleeing for his life from the brother he had cheated, he dedicated his life to God, asking for protection, food and clothes in return (Genesis 28:20). Fifteen years later, returning to his homeland to face Esau he prayed: 'I am unworthy of all the kindness and faithfulness you have shown your servant. I had only this staff when I crossed the Jordan, but now I have become two groups.' (He was by then the wealthy head of two families.) God gives abundantly to those who are worthy of his trust, sometimes in material wealth, sometimes in other less tangible ways. Solomon observed: 'When God gives any man wealth and possessions, and enables him to enjoy them, to accept his lot and be happy in his work – this is a gift of God' (Ecclesiastes 5:19). The key is to seek God's will and to use whatever we have in accordance with that will. Jesus said of material needs: 'But seek first his kingdom and his righteousness, and all these things will be given to you as well' (Matthew 6:33).

Chapter Two

THE BIBLICAL PRINCIPLES
OF GIVING

When they left the church after the first of Robert's sermons, the Silverspoons smiled as they always did while shaking his hand. The birds were singing, and the buds breaking. Spring was in the air, God was in his heaven and Mrs Silverspoon was glowing, resplendent in a dress from one of the finest spring collections.

'What a thought-provoking sermon, Vicar,' she murmured waspishly. 'You must be so glad you have a parish where people are so generous to the church and able to rally round when things need repairing. Can we assume that the PCC are about to appeal for more funds?' Without waiting for a reply she swept magnificently down the path to the churchyard gate, acknowledging a few polite smiles from other members of the congregation with a regal wave. Major Silverspoon followed, discreetly awaiting a suitable moment when he could overtake. He didn't like to barge past while his wife was progressing, but he had to get to the car first, otherwise she would have to wait while he unlocked and opened her door.

Roger Wheldon, a young engineer whose wife had just had a baby, smiled at the one-sided exchange and Robert's gaze at the designer-clad back. 'Mrs S feeling suitably chastised, I see. What does it feel like to have a licence to offend?'

'Unbelievable,' Robert replied, using an expression to cover anything all ways while pondering why some people come to church. Concluding sadly that God wasn't very high on everyone's list he turned to Roger: 'I trust you're not taking umbrage. How's Margaret?'

'Of course I'm not offended. As for Maggie, a week flat on her back has done wonders. The doctor reckons she'll be up again in a few days, thank the Lord.'

'Indeed we should. By the way, when I popped in to see her on Thursday she told me that you should be on the thank-you list too. It can't be easy looking after little James and an immobile wife.'

It's not a problem I'd have by choice, no,' Roger agreed, 'but she's nearly over it now. Just "light duties" for a bit. By the way, thanks for going to trouble of preparing this study' guide,' he flourished a copy collected from the pile Robert had left at the back of the church. 'Maggie was saying that she was sorry to miss one of your specials.'

'I have to admit I really wrote it so that all my hard work didn't go in one ear and out the other. Do tell your good lady that I hope she'll be able to make it next Sunday. If you thought this morning's romp through God's opinion on money was controversial, wait till we look at some specifics about using the stuff!' And so Robert wrote . . .

'. . . OF YOUR OWN DO WE GIVE YOU'

In the previous section we looked at God's attitude to money itself and some of the attitudes he expects from his stewards. Christian money management in action revolves round investing in God's work, one of the central aspects being giving. There are certain principles that can be learned from Scripture.

Grace, not law

'For it is by grace you have been saved, through faith – and this not from yourselves, it is the gift of God – not by works, so that no one can boast' (Ephesians 2:8–9). This principle is central in giving, as in all areas of money management. Giving is not motivated by rules laid down by men or religious institutions. We will have to account individually to God for the wealth he has given us. We must decide, in consultation with the Holy Spirit, how God wishes us to use it.

'It's like this. I throw all my money up into the air and what God wants, he keeps. The rest is mine!'

Give oneself first, then money

Paul wrote to the Romans: '. . . offer your bodies as living sacrifices, holy and pleasing to God – this is your spiritual act of worship. Do not conform any longer to the pattern of this world, but be transformed by the renewing of your mind' (Romans 12:1–2). He implies that the Christian faith is not confined to turning up to services. To serve God is to allow him to take control of our lives, including our finances. He will then renew our minds so that we are free to follow him, instead of being enslaved to the acquisition, storage and disposal of money.

In 2 Corinthians Paul describes this principle operating in the Macedonian church. 'Entirely on their own, they urgently pleaded with us for the privilege of sharing in this service to the saints. And they did not do as we expected, but they gave themselves first to the Lord and then to us in keeping with God's will' (2 Corinthians 8:3–5).

Giving is sowing

'Whoever sows sparingly will also reap sparingly, and whoever sows generously will reap generously' (2 Corinthians 9:6). God gives in abundance to those who allow him to use their lives and resources. This is hardly surprising. We all prefer good investments. God likes investing in people who operate in accordance to his principles. The master in the parable of the talents (Luke 19:11–27) took the talent away from the faithless servant, giving it to the one who had demonstrated his understanding of and obedience to the master's priorities. Sowing is also something that comes before reaping. No one would be foolish enough to expect an unmade and unlit fire to provide heat, an unseeded field to grow crops or an unmade investment to yield a return. How often does the church pray for results from its work, then just sit back and do no work?

Seed is wasted if it is planted in the wrong place or neglected while the new plants are growing, as any gardener can testify. He could also tell you that the results take time. God's work isn't completed overnight, any more than plants or people grow up overnight. 'Let us not become weary in doing good, for at the proper time we will reap a harvest if we do not give up' (Galatians 6:9).

Giving is a part of worship

The Old Testament shows us that God intended giving to be a part of worship. During his instructions for the Feast of Unleavened Bread he says, 'No one is to appear before me empty-handed' (Exodus 23:15). The Feast of Harvest is to be celebrated '. . . with the firstfruits of the crops you sow in your field' (Exodus 23:16). The Psalmist echoes this: 'Ascribe to the Lord the glory due his name; bring an offering and come into his courts' (Psalm 96:8). The principle is clear. Work done during the week, and the results of it, were important to God. Formal worship was not something isolated from our work. It included elements of the work done for God during the rest of the week, not least the first share of the fruits that God had given to each worshipper.

There is an old attitude in the church that the 'smallest silver coin' goes in the plate. The average congregation's regular giving to God is a minute fraction of the amount they receive from him. We often teach our children to maintain the tradition by giving them small change to give, but if they did not earn it, it is of little value to them. In the light of the Bible's teaching on giving, are we 'tipping' God? And what are our children learning from watching us?

TITHING: SETTING ASIDE THE FIRST TENTH FOR GOD

Tithing – setting aside for God, in cash or kind, the first tenth of one's income – has been for many people a part of their response to God. In Old English 'tithe' meant 'tenth'. It is in many respects the starting point for stewardship of our wealth.

Tithing's biblical origins go back at least as far as Abraham. His nephew Lot was captured by the kings of Elam, Goiim,

Shinar, and Ellasar. Abraham pursued them to Hobah, routed them in battle and released Lot, his household and a considerable amount of booty. On his return from the battle Abraham met Melchizedek, the king of Salem, and a priest of God (Genesis 14:17ff).

The significance of Melchizedek is explained in the letter to the Hebrews (Hebrews 6:20; 7:1–28): 'Jesus . . . has become a high priest forever, in the order of Melchizedek.' In the letter Melchizedek is said to be a foreshadowing of the Messiah himself. The writer continues: 'He met Abraham returning from the defeat of the kings and blessed him, and Abraham gave him a tenth of everything. First, his name means "king of righteousness"; then also, "king of Salem" means "king of peace" . . . like the Son of God he remains a priest forever' (Hebrews 7:1–3).

Melchizedek is the first mention in Scripture of priesthood in the sense that Jesus is a priest. Tithing is established at the same time: 'Even the patriarch Abraham gave him a tenth of the plunder' (Hebrews 7:4). This tithe to God through Melchizedek is a sign of his commitment to God.

Jacob, too, promised God a tenth of everything (Genesis 28:20). Our tenths are given to Jesus as a mark of our commitment to him. In Scripture, of course, tithing was only the beginning. The people of Israel were also expected to make additional offerings on top. Jesus taught: 'Give and it will be given to you . . . For with the measure you use, it will be measured to you' (Luke 6:38). It is very easy to estimate the cost of doing God's will in advance and only obey him if the costs are going to be met from proven resources. Jesus singled out the poor widow who gave generously despite her poverty as an example of obedience (Luke 21:1–4). The early church didn't count the cost of doing God's will, they just went and carried it out, assuming God would provide whatever was needed. The policy produced huge profits for God. Despite our wealth we often try to work out if we can afford to do God's will first. Since we cannot see the future, we cannot see God's blessings waiting for us and dare not take the risk. As a result, we often don't even start doing God's work, and perhaps we are often poorer materially as a result. Maybe the widow was so poor she couldn't afford *not* to give! 'But seek first his kingdom . . . and all these things will be given to you as well,' said Jesus (Matthew 6:33).

The writer of Hebrews also pointed out that 'the covenant of which he (Jesus) is mediator is superior to the old one' (Hebrews 8:6). The old covenant 'written on tablets of stone' gave laws to be followed religiously, requiring legally-enforcable giving to the priesthood. We now live to serve Jesus as our priest, and the law is 'written on our hearts', so legal enforcement has ceased. But if God has given us a better covenant, should we give him less?

Perhaps Wesley came up with a practical approach for Christians who are worried by tithing as being too legalistic. He analysed his income and decided how much he needed to live to a standard he considered suitable for a servant of God. He didn't tithe because he didn't consider himself bound by the old covenant rules. Instead he gave away everything he earned above the amount which he decided he needed. His account books, which he kept meticulously, show that his giving amounted to a considerable fortune, possibly equivalent to millions today. Perhaps the modern way to apply biblical principles today could be encapsulated in Wesley's phrase: 'Work as hard as you can, earn as much as you can, give away as much as you can.'

Chapter Three

PRACTICAL APPROACHES
TO GIVING

Steve Storey sat in his designer suit, portable phone by his side, staring at the vestry cupboard and feeling that God was giving him a hard time. Robert, again in his favourite armchair, waited patiently as Steve fought with the Holy Spirit. He could imagine the pain the young man was experiencing, perhaps for the first time at this intensity: the 'refining fire' as the New Testament so eloquently put it. He had been there himself. On the other hand, he felt, it was about time. Steve was valuable to God, talented and blessed with many gifts. If only Steve would stop running away.

Never convinced of the value of education, Steve had no formal qualifications. Part of Britain's 'brutalized peasantry', he had left school with only common sense, lots of personality, and the ability to work hard and well when motivated. Why the education system had failed to spot and develop even one talent was a mystery to Robert, one encountered with sickening regularity amongst the inmates of local schools. Convinced that no one was interested in him, Steve had spent the few years since school on ventures of dubious wisdom and occasionally doubtful ethics – anything but follow his more compliant classmates into wage slavery, as he thought. The only factor common to all the ventures was a promise of easy money. Occasionally the promise was fulfilled but somehow the money vanished, usually in ways Steve referred to as 'bad luck'.

Robert and Steve got on well. A young man striving for security and acceptance, Steve welcomed the sanctuary of Robert's vestry in which he felt able to relax his image for a while. The contempt of a press-ganged RE student for 'Bible-bashers' had grown over the years into respect for Robert as another committed fighter, albeit for a different cause, and then into a friendship. Robert's door was usually open but Steve always asked whether it was convenient to call. Robert often wished the worthies of the parish would take the same trouble.

Steve was also impressed by Robert's quiet self-assurance. Why was the only Christian he knew so different from the insipidness that school and church had taught him was characteristic of Christianity? He had come to church to listen to the teaching and found that he could see the sham religion he and Robert both despised ingrained in the congregation. He wondered how Robert could stand it. Then he noticed Robert treating them the same way he had been treated, quietly teaching them about Jesus, tolerating the posing, the anger and the back-biting. Steve even saw Jesus changing people. Then, last Christmas, disgusted by the thought of yet another fix of greed and trivia, Steve spent the holiday with Jesus instead, finally obeying his command to turn from his old ways. Now, a few months later, he was discovering the cost of that commitment!

Steve drew a deep breath: 'So what exactly is God after then, Bob? Does he seriously expect me to give all my money to the poor like the guy in your sermon?'

Robert winced inwardly for the umpteenth time at the abbreviation of his name then considered the question for a moment or two.

'I can't give a yes or no because I have no special revelation from the Almighty about your money. Frankly I have enough trouble listening to him about mine!' They both laughed and Steve relaxed a little.

'How do I talk to him?'

'I can help you to understand the principles God lays down in Scripture to guide you, and I can suggest questions you might usefully discuss with him. Then commit that part of your life to him in prayer, listen to God's answers and make your own decisions.' Robert paused, seeing doubt written on Steve's face. 'Don't look so worried. God will make sure you hear him. Just be honest with him. He's guided lots of us before.'

'So where do I start?'

'You need to be systematic. First of all you can't really ignore the source of your income. If you're working on things that don't honour God, you can hardly expect his blessing, can you?'

'You think my job's wrong?'

'Examine where your money comes from and decide for yourself. I've prepared a little questionnaire that should help you get things into perspective. Galatians 6:9 is a relevant verse: "Let us not become weary in doing good, for at the proper time we will reap a harvest if we do not give up."'

'The questionnaire. Is it just for me?'

'No, not at all. I've had this conversation with about half a dozen other people so far!'

WORKING TO HONOUR GOD

If Jesus had been born in Cheltenham to respectable church people perhaps he would have been a doctor, since surveys show Christians believe medicine is the most 'Christian' occupation. Why? Because it helps people in need without exploiting them. Does God agree? Well his son was brought up in Nazareth, socially equivalent to a council estate. Nor did he escape to become a respectable man of medicine. Jesus ran a carpentry business, making profits from the same community in which he grew up, until the start of his public ministry.

In doing so he lived a perfect and blameless life, righteous enough to be the scapegoat for the whole of humanity. What does this tell us about the gap between our society's attitude to work and profit and God's?

Religious people sometimes try to create God in their own image. Our work can be characterized by a great divorce. We have 'full-time Christian work', performed by saintly people like clergy and missionaries. Because they are working for God their satisfaction is spiritual so we would not let them become 'oppressed by wealth, care and pleasure' by paying normal salary levels. The rest of the people in church on Sunday sell working days to an employer because their priority is the material well-being of their families. This image is one root of some of the major problems facing churches today. Training resources are concentrated on elites and lay people think ministry is the responsibility of the full-timers. Add ignorance, confusion and tradition and you arrive at bloodletting over lay and women's ministry and so on.

This divorce also affects our attitude to the work people do. How many can get up in the morning with the freedom to say to God, 'Good morning, what will we do today?' Most of us just groan, 'Oh God, it's morning.' Our material lives, the jobs we do, the neighbourhoods we inhabit, are priorities we often fit God around. Michael Baughen, the Bishop of Chester, told of a clergyman who turned down a parish in the Wirral because his wife wouldn't live on Merseyside. How many of us would give up material advancement, extra salary or promotion because they would interfere with our 'part-time' ministry? Are we here to worship and serve God, or just idol-rich? Is there such a thing as 'part-time' ministry?

Our work is a gift from God and should be done for God, even if he has seen fit to place us somewhere unpleasant. Shouldn't that work, part of our worship for God, honour him? Immediately we run into difficult decisions. It is easy for example to tell a brother that his work selling heroin to school-children is both illegal and dishonours God (in Malachi 1:6–8 the prophet talks about blemished sacrifices). But what of the employee of a building society whose salary is paid out of profits which are preserved in part by repossessing the homes of people who can't pay their debts?

Nehemiah 5 also poses questions for people investing with such institutions.

Solomon contrasts two workers: 'It is good and proper for a man to eat and drink, and to find satisfaction in his toilsome labour . . . Moreover when God gives any man wealth and possessions, and enables him to enjoy them, to accept his lot and be happy in his work – this is a gift of God' (Ecclesiastes 5:18–19). The alternative, he suggests, is when 'God gives a man wealth, possessions and honour, so that he lacks nothing his heart desires, but God does not enable him to enjoy them, and a stranger enjoys them instead' (Ecclesiates 6:2). Throughout the Bible, God makes it clear that he gives work as a gift to enable people to enjoy their waking hours and care for their families. In return for working they should be paid in full (Deuteronomy 25:4) and on time (24:15).

Does this only apply to employees? Our industrial society has made the concept of lifetime employment much more normal than it was in the past. The labourers referred to in the Bible tended to be employed on a daily basis, apart from full-time slaves and, perhaps, the king's courtiers, officials and professional soldiers. In today's terms, most people would have been self-employed. Perhaps profit might be an appropriate term. The great divorce between work and our lives for God shouldn't exist. Our work is a worthy and legitimate form of worship unless we are unfairly or immorally exploiting someone. We therefore deserve to profit in full. That might be in terms of salary, profits or royalties.

What should our attitude as neighbours be to workers? The work divorce often leads us to compartmentalize such matters away from our social, home and church lives. When friends approach us to sell us something it leaves a nasty taste, but why? If we knew we wanted to buy something, wouldn't we support a friend's business if he could provide the item at a competitive price? So why do we get upset if someone who knows (because it's his job) of an item we don't and suggests we might like to try it?

This will become a particular issue with the growth of networking as a means of distribution. Of course, if the business is not reputable, the products don't work, or the approach is clearly inappropriate or exploitative then we have a right to be upset. If not, doesn't someone making an honest living serving his community in a way God has given him deserve at least a fair hearing? Aren't we all trustworthy enough to hear and tell the truth in love, even if the truth is 'No, thanks'? The bad taste doesn't come from the profits, the fruits of our work are a gift from God. It's more likely the result of a shock against our culture's attitude to profit, a shock which is only really appropriate if profit comes from more questionable sources.

The same applies to the business opportunities provided by such programmes. If you fell into a goldmine and needed help to carry away the treasure, would you advertise for strangers or tell your friends? What would you think if your friends didn't tell you?

Use the 'Working to honour God' questionnaire.

A few days later Steve popped his head round the vestry door and found Robert struggling with a desk piled high with papers.

'Have you got a tick?'

'Sure, take a seat. I need a break from this rubbish.' Robert eyed the mess with distaste. 'Some paperwork in the church is inevitable I suppose, but if I'd wanted to be a bureaucrat I'd have become a civil servant. Anyway, How did you get on?'

'I'm having a bit of a career rethink at the moment, but I haven't finished yet.'

'I'd be worried if you felt you had sorted it out in three days.'

'But what about tithing though?' asked Steve. 'That's why I originally came to see you.'

'I haven't forgotten,' replied Robert, 'But having started with the means of production, so to speak, you're better able to look at the allocation of resources aren't you?'

'You reckon tithe a tenth, eh?'

'Is God telling you otherwise?'

'I suppose not. It just seems a heck of a lot, with taxes and all.'

WORKING TO HONOUR GOD
A questionnaire on our attitudes to working

1. Does my career or profession exemplify the Christian life?

2. If my colleagues accused me of being a Christian because of my work habits, would they have any evidence?

3. Is it possible for me to honour God in my work?

4. Does the organization I work for observe biblical standards when dealing with customers, clients and other members of the public, eg local residents?

5. Am I making others violate my own principles?

6. Two verses to measure our work by:

'Do not lie to each other, since you have taken off your old self with its practices' (Colossians 3:9).

'The righteous care about justice for the poor, but the wicked have no such concern' (Proverbs 29:7).

'Malachi 3:8. "Will a man rob God? Yet you rob me." When Israel asked how they were robbing God he said: "In tithes and offerings. You are under a curse – the whole nation of you – because you are robbing me. Bring the whole tithe into the storehouse, that there may be food in my house".'

'Doesn't pull his punches, does he?' observed Steve.

'No. But then he says: "See if I will not throw open the floodgates of heaven and pour out so much blessing that you will not have room enough for it."'

'Sounds like it would be daft to short-change him.'

'Quite,' agreed Robert, 'but don't think you can force God to make you rich by giving. Remember the Pharisees? They tithed literally everything. Jesus still called them a brood of vipers because of their attitude. Look at James 4:3. "When you ask, you do not receive, because you ask with wrong motives, that you may spend what you get on your pleasures." It's the attitude behind the giving that is really important.'

'So giving less is OK if your attitude is right?'

'If your attitude is right would you want to give less?'

'OK. Ten per cent then,' decided Steve. 'Was there income tax in the Bible?'

'That's a roundabout way of asking if tithes come from gross earnings or net, right?'

'Spot on.'

'Well, in those days part of the tithe went to help the poor and things like that. Nowadays there's much more state provision, so there's a case for saying you tithe net, but then the state system is part of our own insurance if we became sick, widowed, unemployed or whatever. I don't see a scriptural case to leave welfare provision entirely to the state, especially as there's plenty it doesn't do. Nor are insurance premiums tithe-deductible, as far as I can see. On balance I would say ten per cent of gross.' Steve looked a little pained. 'But you could give gross and pay net.'

'How?' said Steve guardedly.

'Covenant your tithes!' said Robert triumphantly.

'Do what?'

'Suppose you earn a thousand pounds. Your tithe is one hundred. Now suppose you pay twenty-five per cent tax. If you covenant £75, the tax man gives the church the twenty-five pounds tax you paid on it. Your tithe has become a hundred pounds again.'

'Neat,' said Steve, his eyes sparkling at the simplicity. 'You ever thought of being an accountant?'

'Yes, but it's much more fun being a pastor.'

'And the rest is mine?'

'Yours to manage, yes.'

'Can I spend it any way I like?'

'You're the one accountable to God.' Robert pulled a booklet from a file on his desk and handed it to Steve. 'The church treasurer put together a little guide for me. It covers covenants, lump sum giving like Gift Aid, and so on.'

Steve grinned. 'Don't tell me. You've given a few of these away too.'

'You've heard of the six Ps, haven't you? Preparation and Planning Prevents Pathetically Poor Performance!' As Steve, still chuckling, got up to leave, Robert added, 'Oh, and once you've sorted out your giving, can I suggest a budget now you're managing part of God's work. You wouldn't try to run your own business without one, would you?'

THE GOOD GIVING GUIDE

Once you've decided to give part of your income to God for his work there are a number of simple ways to do it. Money is fairly easy because it is the form of wealth that most people receive and systems are available to handle it. Givers of non-cash items, such as property, may like to discuss the situation with their church elders or parish council. Professional advice may also be needed with tax and similar matters. 'Income' obviously includes wages and salaries, but it may also be appropriate to give parts of lump sums like inheritances.

Some Christians may feel that the church they belong to is itself likely to misuse the money and perhaps should only receive part of the money, although this decision should only be taken after prayer since God has ordained that our ministry should be through the church. This is only really a problem in churches who have long since lost any vision for the Holy

Spirit's work and spend most of their money on things like the church buildings or religious finery. Before diverting funds, though, try to donate something the Spirit can use in that church: for instance, a training library, resources for the youth group, or finance for a missionary.

If all else fails, alternative recipients are a matter of individual conscience again. In principle, if the gift is to God the money should be given to some part of the Body of Christ, a specifically Christian ministry, for example. Gifts to our own favourite secular charities should perhaps be from our own money, not God's.

REGULAR GIVING

Covenanted giving

Covenants are the most tax-effective method of regular giving from taxpayers. It provides the long term predictable income which your church needs to function properly and delivers maximum spending power from your gift. It is simply a legally binding agreement to give away part of your income every year. Most churches and charities have covenant forms available upon request. (Most church treasurers will become instant friends if you ask!) Most church covenants run for four years but provide escape clauses if your circumstances change and you cannot continue.

Major denominations will be registered as charities and able to reclaim the tax earned on covenanted gifts already. Some of the smaller churches, especially house churches, should also consider such status. The Charity Commission at Haymarket, London W1 can provide advice. Tax is reclaimed from the Claims Branch (Charity Division), HM Inspector of Taxes, St John's House, Merton Road, Stanley Precinct, Bootle, Merseyside L69 9BB. Tel: 051–922 6363.

The spending power advantage comes when the church claims back the income tax you paid. If you give £75 a month, say, then the charity can claim another £25 from the taxman, making £100 in all, assuming the income tax base rate is twenty-five per cent. The church takes care of all the paperwork. If you are a higher rate taxpayer, just insert the details in the box provided on your tax return and your tax office will arrange for you to receive the additional relief, usually through your tax coding.

Do remember that this type of giving can only be used by those who pay income tax. If you are not a taxpayer then it will be simpler just to give money straight to the church. This also applies to couples where only one partner pays tax. The covenant should be made in the name of the taxpaying spouse, otherwise the church will collect tax that has not been paid!

If you make a joint covenant then you are treated as paying half each, unless you can show that you make unequal payments. This means that you may well pay more tax than you should if one spouse pays higher rate tax and the other pays only base rate.

How to give by covenant

This depends on the church. You may pay in cash or cheque, or by direct debit.

Cash or cheque giving
Most churches run an envelope giving scheme. Put the amount you've agreed into the envelope and give it through the collection plate. Remember that you have made a commitment to give that amount each week or month.

Direct transfer
If you have a church with a bank account, ask the treasurer for a standing order or direct debit mandate. Once this is presented, your bank will pay the agreed amount into the church's account. Such instructions can be stopped or changed at any time by written instruction. Standing orders are very common but will need to be replaced completely every time you change your giving amount (eg when your annual salary changes).

If your church isn't a charity and/or doesn't have a bank account, best use may not be being made of available resources (especially if the treasurer is running the church accounts out of a cash box). There is also a risk from theft. Suggest that a bank account be opened, even if only for safety's sake.

There are also some schemes set up to finance any charity, not just the church.

Payroll Giving Schemes

These are operated by some employers. The recipients benefit by receiving the tax normally paid on the money. They rely on the employer's cooperation since you cannot insist that your employer runs a scheme. Again they are very simple. You tell your employer to deduct an amount from your wages each payday. The employer than passes it to an agency charity, who give it to the charity of your choice. It is taken from you before tax is deducted and so goes to the charity in full.

The most you can give in any one year by this method at present is £480 a year. A couple who both pay tax may give £480 a year each. You may stop payment at any time, subject to any minimum notice period your employer may need, but any payments that are made and given tax relief must go to charity.

Obviously you cannot get two sets of tax relief on the same money by using both schemes, but there is nothing to stop you simultaneously having a covenant for one part of your giving, and a payroll scheme for different part.

Further details on 'Tax Aid' are given in a leaflet published by the Inland Revenue (IR65), available from your tax office, or any Tax Enquiry Centre. There is also a leaflet, IR64, which explains how businesses can give to charity and obtain tax relief.

One-off gifts

'Gift Aid' allows individuals or businesses to give single cash sums of over £400 to charities with full tax relief. It operates like Tax Aid. The donor gives the money and a certificate (R190(SD) from individual donors and R240(SD) from companies). The recipient then reclaims tax paid on the gift. The upper limit should not worry many people since you can give up to £5,000,000 a year in this way.

A £400 gift will, after reclaim of tax, be worth £533.33 in the hands of the recipient, and higher-rate tax payers will again receive back any higher rate tax they paid on the money.

Full details are given in the Inland Revenue Booklet IR113 'Gift Aid: A Guide for Donors and Charities', available from your Tax Office or Tax Enquiry Centre.

Chapter Four

BUDGETING

Roger Wheldon refilled the three glasses on the table between them and put the wine bottle back in the ice bucket. He looked at Margaret, his wife, and then back to Robert. 'Mostly we just wonder where it all goes! Since Maggie gave up work to have James there's always been a bit too much month at the end of the money, so to speak.'

'To be honest,' said Margaret, thoughtfully, 'it would be nice to be in control of our money and not money in charge of us. And we had absolutely no idea that God was even interested in it.'

'I can't say I'm surprised to hear that,' Robert replied. 'We're all supposed to "look after Number One" and as a result everything revolves around us, including God. We think he can wait for us to give him whatever we've got spare. Most of us run our time, our ambitions, careers, probably every aspect of our lives that way, not just our money.'

'Seek first the Kingdom of Man, and anything left over can be given to God,' Margaret paraphrased the Sermon on the Mount, much to Robert's amusement.

'I must use that line in a sermon. How wonderfully Aristotelian!'

'Aristo–what?' queried Roger, philosophy not being his major suit.

'Aristotle believed that Earth was the centre of the universe and all the heavens rotated round us on a series of glass "celestial spheres". Of course Galileo and Copernicus worked out that the earth isn't the centre of the universe. Funny how modern man lives as though God revolves around *him*.' Robert pushed the historical analogy further. 'You could see Jesus as a sort of Galileo, telling us that God is at the centre of the system, whereas modern scientific man is like Aristotle, still in the dark ages, believing in a flat earth surrounded by glass balls!'

'So your sermons aim to get people to run their money assuming we revolve around God, not him around us?' asked Roger.

'That's about right. We serve him, not the other way round. Our money is his. As his managers we answer to him for what we do with it.'

'I'm amazed that he's not more angry about how we use it, then,' commented Margaret.

'Indeed, but look at it like this. You give young James toys and games, don't you? But how long is it before they're broken?'

'Not long!' she laughed.

'Precisely. Does that stop you loving him? No. Does that stop you giving him things? No. You love him and you want to see him enjoying himself. And without those things he wouldn't learn and develop properly anyway. But I bet you also try to teach him to use them properly and not to take you or them for granted.'

'So what you're saying is God is teaching us to behave more responsibly, but accepts that we're bound to break a few toys while we're learning. Any suggestions about reducing the damage?' asked Margaret.

'*That* is between you and God. I don't make the rules. But you could start with a proper budget, which will allow you to make informed decisions about where the money's going. One of the delights of living on a vicar's stipend is that Catherine and I need to account for practically every penny or ends don't meet.'

Roger's face fell a little. 'I don't think we're disciplined enough for that. I find it an effort to keep track of the cheque book stubs! I'm so busy earning the stuff, I don't have time.'

'Roger! you wimp!' scolded Margaret in jest. 'I didn't sacrifice my career to bear your child only to discover that you can't even be bothered to balance the cheque book!'

'Well, someone's got to earn the money!' he retorted. 'I'm happy to be in the decision-making team, but since you're lying around all day at home why don't you run the paper-work?'

Margaret smiled mischievously. 'You earn it. I'll spend it! Sounds a wonderful idea to me, darling! I'll start first thing in the morning.' Turning to Robert she asked, 'Where did you and Catherine begin?'

'We isolated three areas of cash-flow. The first is giving God his share. Then providing for your material needs. Paul told Timothy: "If anyone does not provide for his relatives, and especially for his immediate family, he has denied the faith and is worse than an unbeliever" (1 Timothy 5:8).'

'How far does "immediate family" extend?' asked Roger.

'How long is a piece of string? Obviously it covers the three of you, but you'd probably upset God if you ignored any relative in trouble if God had given you the resources to help. "Material needs" includes things you need for living. Food, clothes, accommodation, insurance, transport, all that stuff.'

'What do you mean by "need"?' asked Roger, sensing another grey area.

'Without it you can't live properly, although inevitably that will vary between people. Catherine and I started by listing everything we bought and marked each thing as "essential", "desirable" or "luxury".'

'But how did you decide?'

'Well, suppose you need a car. It might be "essential" to have a good used car. If you have enough cash and nothing more urgent to use it for, you may "desire" a new one. If God has really blessed you he may let you buy a "luxury" like a new Lotus.'

'That rule probably applies to everything from food to holidays.'

'It does, but try to avoid false economies. We go for best value for money instead of cheapest, given the choice.'

'That's obvious, isn't it?'

'You'd be amazed how many people feel super-spiritual about buying cheap stuff which they're always replacing, when a bit of planning and shrewd shopping would save money in the long run. Are you in debt?'

'Well, only the mortgage. We've even paid off the credit cards.'

'Good. I suggest you keep it that way. If you had debts I would suggest putting a special section into the budget for repaying them and bringing you back into credit. In your case if you've anything left over it'll come under the third of our categories: surplus.'

'I don't think we'll have much of that, Robert,' giggled Margaret.

'We were surprised how much we were wasting before we budgeted,' replied Robert, 'especially if you classify luxury spending as coming from "surplus". Most people spend money without even thinking and wonder why they feel they can't meet their own priorities in life. I think you might be surprised how quickly taking control of your money helps bring you into a "positive cash-flow situation", as the bankers might say.'

'The effect of regular pay rises, I suppose?' said Roger.

'If you're in control of outgoings, obviously increased income will help in time. But the knowledge of what you buy itself gives you the choice of diverting the cash elsewhere. Accumulating surplus cash is tremendously useful. In Bible times it provided for lean periods. Today that could be anything from repairing sudden breakages to coping with long-term sickness or redundancy, although insurance plays a role there too. And most luxuries like nicer holidays may come out of saving a surplus. Certainly the Bible discourages the use of credit for purchases.'

'Save first, then spend?' asked Margaret.

'Absolutely. Then God might occasionally ask you to give it to those in need rather than spend it on yourselves. Paul commends the Macedonian church who gave from poverty, and suggests to the Corinthians that they should be generous givers: "At the present time your plenty will supply what they need, so that in turn their plenty will supply what you need" (2 Corinthians 8:14). There are times when rich Christians are needed for large scale investment. I know one businessman whose ministry is making money, building up surpluses and giving them away.'

'That's not tithing, though, is it?' Roger queried.

'No, that's in addition to his tithes.'

'So we build up surpluses after we've tithed?'

'If you've got any spare cash.'

'And the tithe is ten per cent?'

'That's the biblical norm, but you need to ask God how much he wants of your money. All I can say is he doesn't go a bundle on people who give him tips.'

MAKING A HOUSEHOLD BUDGET

Budgeting simply aims to match your total spending with your income. Overspending erodes your savings or forces you to borrow. If you borrow you will have even less money to spend in the future. Budgeting works by letting you decide in advance how much to spend on given items and then helps you monitor the spending. When you can see how much money is available you can tell in advance the effect that changing spending plans will have. This allows you to prioritize spending on the most important items.

Curiously enough, the most important reason why people don't budget is fear of knowing where the money goes. To overcome that fear start with the attitude that you're looking for wasted money to divert to something that's important to you. If necessary, promise yourself a little reward for success.

Step one

What do you earn? Using Table 4.1 list all your sources of income. If you pay tax under the Pay As You Earn system (PAYE or Schedule E), income tax and other stoppages are taken at source so enter the actual amount you receive. If you're paid in full (self-employed earnings, rents etc), subtract an allowance for tax and National Insurance and enter whatever is left. Remember any government benefits that you receive and check that you are getting everything you're entitled to.

Step two

Make a list of everything that you spend. If you keep receipts, bills and so on, check them. If not, make the best estimate that you can and don't forget to allow for inflation, especially if the spending records you have are old! Be honest at this stage: don't pretend you spend less than you do. We will come to prioritizing spending later. Table 4.2 lists most of the items that make up a normal household budget.

You will find that there are three sorts of everyday expenditure. Mark each item according to how important the item is:

Essentials like mortgage payments or rent, utility bills like gas, food, clothes, insurance premiums and so forth.

TABLE 4.1 YOUR INCOME

All figures should be inserted NET (ie after stoppages, or an allowance for income tax and national insurance)

Type of income	Amount per week/month £
Wages/salary—your pay:	
overtime/bonus/ commission/profits, etc	
your partner's pay	
overtime/bonus/ commission/profits, etc	
Part-time jobs	
Benefits:	
Social security	
Sickness benefit	
Family income supplement	
Family credit	
Child benefit	
Unemployment benefit	
Housing benefit	
Disability benefits	
Other	
Maintenance payments	
Retirement pension	
Occupational pension	
Other pensions	
Any other income, investments, lodgers, etc	
TOTAL NET INCOME:	

Desirables such as saving and expenditure like TVs, newspapers, entertainment and holidays, which are important but which can be reduced or even eliminated if money gets tight.

Luxuries like drink, tobacco, luxury consumer durables, extra clothes and other items which you probably only buy if you don't need the money for something more important.

Remember to take account of things which include significant 'downstream' costs. For example, a car will need insuring, petrol, servicing and tax. If you're planning to buy one, remember to make sure your budget can stand the strain of running it. The same may apply to items like cable TV subscriptions, new CD players, second homes etc.

Once you've decided how important different items are, you can see if your income covers that expenditure. You may be in for a pleasant surprise and find you have a surplus which can be saved. Look out for spending which, with thought and planning, can be eliminated. Budgeting becomes worthwhile when you find spare money for something you've always wanted but thought you couldn't afford.

Of course you may find you're short of income. Then you will have to make some decisions about which items are going to be cut out or reduced. The job will be easier now you have decided how important individual items are.

Step three

You now have the delightful task of monitoring the spending to keep to the budget. You could keep everything in cash and keep it in a series of pots dedicated to each item, but cash does have certain disadvantages: most bills come quarterly; insurance premiums tend to be monthly or yearly. Perhaps most important is that thieves like cash but the companies sending bills tend not to. A small 'float' kept in a proper cash-box is useful for odd purchases if you run out of something or for paying the papers or the milk.

The simple solution is to run things through a bank account. Income is paid in, and bills are paid out by cheque. Cash can be withdrawn by cheque or cashcards, or you can use the

TABLE 4.2 MONTHLY/WEEKLY EXPENDITURE

1. Housekeeping
Food
Cleaning materials
Pet foods
Laundry
Other

Total housekeeping:

2. Everyday spending
Baby maintenance
Children's pocket money
Childminding/babysitting
Toys and books
Medicines (including prescriptions)
Motor fuel
Parking
Fares
TV and video rental
Hobbies
Records and tapes
Drinks
Tobacco
Newspapers and journals
Other

Total everyday spending:

3. Formal commitments
Property   Mortgage/rents
              Council tax
              Service and maintenance charges
              Building insurance
              Contents insurance
              Other

Services   Electricity
              Gas
              Household fuel
              Telephone
              TV licence and subscriptions

Car	MOT
	Road tax
	Car insurance
	Maintenance

Finance	Tithes
	Other charity and church giving
	Regular savings
	Life assurances
	Other protection plans, PHI, accidents, etc
	Pension provision
	Share option plans
	Maintenance payments
	Second mortgage
	Loan, HP repayments
	Credit card repayments
	School fees
	Other

Total formal commitments:

4. Occasional Costs

Christmas
Birthdays
Holidays
House maintenance and decoration
Clothes
Medical/dental/optical/vet's fees
Trips, outings, meals out
Other

Total formal commitments:

TOTAL MONTHLY/WEEKLY EXPENDITURE:

Note: Items such as protection policies, regular savings and investments, pension provision should all be considered in conjunction with chapter 7 and Table 7.1.

new debit cards like 'Switch'. Whichever you prefer, make sure you have a hard copy master record of the amount of money in your bank account. The simplest way is to keep a running record on your cheque book.

Keep receipts for all purchases (if you're in a hurry these can be stuck in a special wallet, or on a spike) and then set aside some time every week to list all income and spending in a cashbook and keep your cheque book up to date. You can ask the bank to make regular payments by direct debit or standing order. If you do, deduct all such expenditure for the next month from your running balance in advance.

By comparing actual expenditure with your budget regularly, you'll know whether you're overspending, or building up a surplus. If you do make a surplus, pat yourself on the back. Don't be afraid of giving yourself or your family a treat if you're doing really well; it will help keep you motivated!

A simple refinement is to maintain a budget account. These are simply accounts from which only regular bills and standing orders are paid. It's up to you to decide which items are paid from this account. This might include the mortgage or rent, insurances and any utilities and services, like gas and telephones. You may also include holidays, Christmas and birthday expenses, which only turn up annually and can sometimes be forgotten until the last minute. The budget account is funded by a monthly transfer from the main current account. Some clearing banks offer these accounts in a package for this purpose.

Depending on their preferences, couples may wish to keep separate personal accounts for personal spending on surprises for each other, hobbies, socializing with friends, and so on.

Guidelines for selecting a good bank and operating accounts are given later in the chapter.

BANKING ARRANGEMENTS

What makes a good bank account? Regular contact with a friendly bank manager is becoming less common, since his sales targets seem to leave him less time to worry about individual customers unless they're causing him problems. Rich people may be able to qualify for some of the 'private banks' like Adam & Co, but most of us will only be welcome in the familiar high street clearing banks and building societies.

Essential features in a bank account

1. Free statements, monthly standing orders and direct debits, cheque guarantee and cashcards.

2. Interest on positive balances.

3. No limits on number of cheques drawn or amounts on each.

4. No charges if in credit.

5. Good branch network, and widespread access to cashpoints or automated teller machines (ATMs).

Watch out for:

1. Charges levied on accounts that go overdrawn. All banks make them, some are worse than others.

2. Home banking via a computer modem is becoming more common and may suit some people.

3. It can take up to 10 days for cheques to be credited (cleared) to some building society accounts because they're not members of the banks 'clearing system'. It only takes three days for a bank.

4. Debit cards are a common option which many people prefer because they are convenient. Card users should keep a careful record of transactions to avoid unnoticed overspending

5. £100 cheque guarantee cards are useful, but not always available.

Monitoring a bank account

1. Check monthly statements against cheque book stubs and cashpoint or debit card receipts. Make sure the cheque book is up to date at all times

2. Tell the bank *before* you go overdrawn. Unauthorized overdrafts are much more expensive than agreed ones.

3. If you dip into the red by fifty pence just for a day, even by mistake, some banks will collect up to three months' worth of bank charges. If this happens write to the manager explaining what happened and asking if he can waive the charges.

Don't forget to keep cheque cards separate from the cheque book, and Personal Identity Numbers (PINs) secret.

4. Complaints: Make your manager earn his money. Demand a good service and complain if you don't get

'. . . . *says more about you than cash ever can!*'

it. If he cannot sort out any problems to your satisfaction write to his Area, or even Regional, Manager. If that doesn't work, try the Managing Director at Head Office. As a final resort there is a Banking and Building Society Ombudsman. Threatening to move your account, assuming you're a responsible customer, really motivates them to help.

5. Bank staff are human. If they're good or sort out a problem well they like a thank-you as much as you do and are even friendlier next time.

Credit cards

These can really destroy your financial planning. They provide un-monitored spending facilities and can get you into financial bondage (see chapter 5) without you noticing. It's not the card that's a problem, it's the self-discipline, or lack of it, of the person using it. Obey the following rules:

1. Only use the card for budgeted items.

2. Pay the account in full every month, without exception.

3. Destroy the card if you break the rules.

Chapter Five

DEBT

Robert glanced round the living room of Pete and Linda Saunders' small terraced house. The garishly coloured trappings of a new baby clashed with the adult glamour of expensive fixtures and furniture. Together they told of a lavish lifestyle abruptly curtailed by the arrival of what one husband described as 'the most efficient way known to turn money into manure'.

Linda Saunders was not a regular church-goer. In spite of her being a local girl, Robert's only recent contact with her had been through baby David's blessing service a few months earlier. Her requesting his visit had been no less welcome for that, but Robert had been concerned at the faint tone of despair he had detected in her voice. He settled into a leather settee that faced the fire place and waited quietly. He had learned that people in trouble appreciated the opportunity to offer some form of hospitality. Linda made tea.

She was a very attractive twenty-six year old, dressed in black-and-white striped leggings and a baggy white sweater which set off a cascade of red hair. Three gold bracelets adorned her right wrist and an expensive watch her left. She put the mugs on a long low table in front of the settee, then sat on a sheepskin fireside rug facing Robert. As she curled her long legs beneath her, Robert remembered earlier generations often dressing their 'best', hiding the booze, even scattering church magazines around in a generally mistaken belief that visiting clergymen were offended by normal family life. The more relaxed attitude of today's young was a welcome change.

'Thank you very much for phoning, Linda,' he began. 'How's parenthood?'

'We both love it,' Linda's eyes sparkled at the thought. 'Apart from some sleepless nights, David's really fine. We hadn't planned to have kids this fast but we're amazed how much fun it all is. Pete's a really great dad, though my mum still doesn't quite believe me.'

'Sounds like you're off to a fine start,' he said, relieved that wife battering and child abuse obviously weren't on the day's pastoral menu. 'So the slightly desperate sound on the telephone was just maternal overwork?'

Behind her smile a cloud began to gather. 'Not quite. There is something we'd like some advice on. Or rather I would: Pete's a bit embarrassed. I thought you might know where we could talk to someone.' She caught his eye and he could see panic behind the well made-up facade. He said nothing and held her gaze, but she flicked it away and studied the sheepskin closely. Then she mumbled, 'It's a bit embarrassing really. If Mum knew what had happened she'd kill us.'

Knowing Linda's mother, Robert found that hard to believe. He prompted a little. 'I probably know all kinds of people who can help, and confidentially. But I need to know what the problem is.'

'Well, to get this house we took a huge mortgage, which was OK then, but now David's come I can't work . . .' she tailed off. 'I don't think we can manage any more.' She paused again and her voice dropped, 'In fact, I know we can't.'

'Is it just the mortgage?'

'Not really. If that was all, we could just manage. But we had to furnish the place. At first we got a whole load of cast-offs from Mum and Dad but she was always reminding us about it, especially Pete. We got fed up with feeling like beggars. Mum's really sweet, but . . .' She stopped – apparently absorbed again by the rug.

'. . . but sensitivity isn't her strongest suit.' Robert finished the sentence for her. 'I suppose you borrowed heavily to buy all this lovely furniture.'

'That's it really. We could keep up the other loans if both of us were working, but with losing my pay and the extra costs of the baby it's just too much. We can't live and pay everything. And I can't go to Mum, because she'll blame Pete. And there'll be rows . . .' She paused again. 'So I wondered if you knew anybody who knows how we can sort ourselves out. It was when this came that we really panicked.' She stretched up and pulled a letter off the mantelpiece above her. 'It's from a finance company who lent us some money.' She unfolded the letter and passed it to him. As Robert read it she continued, 'That's the first one that's turned nasty so far, but we're behind on the mortgage and the hi-fi payments, and all the credit cards are full. Pete says we can't even make the minimum payments and the bank manager has refused to increase our overdraft.'

'You've already asked him, then?'

'The last two times he said yes, but now he thinks we're in too deep. But that means we're going to go to court.' Her eyes were beginning to glisten. 'In the pub last week the others were talking about your money sermons. I thought you might know what to do. I can't face Mum and Dad, the bank manager won't help and I'm really scared.'

'Does Pete feel the same?' Robert asked.

'Yes. I told him you were coming.'

'Good, because the first step is for you both to agree that you're going to get out of this together. There may or may not be an easy way out but there will be a way out. Could you work, even part-time? Perhaps leave David with his grandparents?'

'We thought about that,' Linda replied, 'but Mum thinks a mother's place is with the baby. She'd keep telling Pete he's not a proper husband, things like that.'

'Ideally you should be with your child. But you aren't exactly in an ideal world, are you? And there are ways of working from home, incidentally.' Without waiting for a reply he continued, injecting a business-like enthusiasm to his voice. 'We have two problems to face. The first is the immediate need to stabilize your position. Right?'

Linda nodded, beginning to respond to Robert's evident belief that her world wasn't about to end. 'What's the second?'

'You keep saying that you can or can't do things because your mother may or not not approve. A lot of your debts seem to come from trying to meet her expectations. Even if she really does expect it, why does it matter what other people say?'

DEALING WITH DEBT: FINANCIAL FIRST AID

If you're in debt you probably won't feel like a detailed analysis of why. You probably know anyway. So let's just start with a plan to stop the problem getting worse and then get you on the road out of debt. Plenty of time later to explore why it happened and stop it happening again.

The sooner you face the problem the easier it will be to solve it. So let's act **now**!

The first rule to follow is: Don't ignore creditors (the people you owe money to) or their letters. Tell them you've a problem. Follow this six-point action plan.

Step one: *Work out your income*

Go to Table 4.1. Use it to find out how much money you have coming in each week or month. Include any benefits you already receive, and contact the Department of Social Security (DSS) to find out if you're entitled to any others. The total amount is your net income.

Step two: *Where does it all go?*

Fill in Table 4.2 as well as you can. Chapter 4 also explains how to determine what is essential spending, and what you can do without if necessary. The better you can do it, the more effective it will be and the easier solving the problem will become. This will show your net expenditure. Then fill in Table 5.1 to clarify how much you owe, and to whom.

Add up all the essentials, including any fixed repayments that you're making. Take that away from the net income and you'll get an amount available for the repayment of the debts.

Step three: Still too much going out?

This is the hard part because sacrifices may be necessary. Look again at what you're spending. Is it really all essential? What else can you do without? Is there anything you can sell to bring in money to pay debts? (**do not** sell anything on which you still owe money. Instead contact the lender to see what terms they can offer to take it back.)

Step four: Can you increase your income?

Contact your Tax Office and make sure you're not paying too much tax. The DSS will advise you on any extra benefits you can claim. Could you get an extra part-time job or work from home?

Step five: What do you owe?

Table 5.1 has given you a complete list of your debts. It should cover all your creditors, the amounts you owe, including arrears (the amount you're behind) on payments if any. Now you need to decide which are most important. Some debts can cause you bigger problems than others and these are priority loans. For example, you could lose your home if your mortgage is foreclosed, or your hi-fi if the finance company repossesses it. Which is more important?

Step six: Talk to your creditors

Send your creditors a financial statement showing your income and outgoings. (Table 5.2 is such a statement.)

TABLE 5.1 WHAT DO YOU OWE?

PRIORITY CREDITORS

Creditor	Payment date	Regular amount (if any)	Arrears
Rent/mortgage			
Gas			
Electricity			
Council tax			
Water			
Others			

OTHER CREDITORS

Bank loans

Hire purchase

Credit cards

Other creditors

Explain, using the statement, how much you need to live on and make them a fair offer to repay the debt. Offer what you can afford. A small regular payment is better than nothing and you must be able to keep up the new payments.

Deal with the priority debts first. Concentrate on keeping the roof over your head.

If you've got several creditors decide how much to offer each one. The amount should reflect the size of the debt, so don't necessarily offer the same to each one.

Ask if the company will 'freeze' interest payments on loans or credit cards. Then you just need to deal with the debt itself.

Don't be put off by unfriendly people. And don't give up. Go higher up the firm.

Keep copies of any letters to and from the companies. Make notes on the contents of all telephone calls, the date and time, and the name of the person you spoke to.

Debt is one of the loneliest places on earth, as you probably already know. Human support and friendship is priceless. Your church may be able to help or put you in touch with someone who can.

On the technical side, the church may know a licensed debt counsellor. A local legal aid solicitor may give you free advice. The Citizen's Advice Bureau may be able to help and will know if there's a Money Advice Centre in your area.

Most reputable lenders prefer to come to a sensible arrangement rather than get nasty. But what if things are already getting out of hand? Obviously individual circumstances will vary, so specific advice here is impossible, but here are two common problems.

'I'm being harassed by creditors!'

There's nothing wrong with a creditor reminding you politely of the debt from time to time. You *cannot*, however, be

TABLE 5.2 YOUR FINANCIAL POSITION

Name
Address

INCOME PER WEEK/MONTH	Amount £
Net earnings	
Benefit incomes	
Other sources	
TOTAL INCOME:	

ESSENTIAL WEEKLY/MONTHLY SPENDING

Rent/mortgage
Council tax
Household insurance
Life assurance
Gas
Electricity
Other fuel
Housekeeping
TV rental
TV licence
Travelling expenses
Clothes
School meals
Other

TOTAL INCOME:

AVAILABLE FOR REPAYING DEBTS
(Income-Expenditure)

I owe money to:

After priority creditors I can offer
to repay each week/month

prosecuted in the criminal court for debt, even if some creditors tell you you can. Call the police, or the local Trading Standards Officers (at your Town Hall) if creditors harass you by: telephoning you late at night; telephoning you repeatedly at work; contacting your employer; making threats or unreasonable demands.

'They're taking me to court'

Don't panic. You'll be treated fairly and you won't go to prison. Go and see a Law Centre or Citizen's Advice Bureau for help with the forms. Briefly this is what should happen:

Fill in the forms and send them back as quickly as possible. If you dispute the claim fill in the 'defence' form. If you agree you owe the money, fill in the 'admission' form. Give details of your income, spending and circumstances. Table 5.2 will help here. Make a realistic offer to repay.

Make sure you attend the hearings. If you don't you may be held 'in contempt of court'. It's always best to put your side of the story. Take the information about your situation. If you want time to pay take evidence to support your request.

The court will send you it's judgment. This will give details of any instalments you are being instructed to pay. If you can't pay off the debt within a month, details of the debt will go onto the public register of County Court Judgements, which will probably affect your ability to get credit in the future.

  If you keep paying the instalments, your goods will not normally be taken away. If your circumstances change, apply to the court for the instalments to be changed (the technical term for this is varied).

Your creditor may ask for the court to take other action. He may get an order seizing any money you have in the bank or building society. If you are working, the court may make an 'attachment of earnings order'. This tells your employer to pay some of your earnings direct to the court. A 'charging order' applies to arrears on a mortgage. If your house is sold in future the company you have your mortgage with will get their money from the proceeds and you will get what's left. Until then you must keep up the mortgage payments or the house could be sold and you evicted.

You could ask the court to help sort out your debts. With a judgment against you and total debts of less than £5,000 you may ask for an 'administration order'. Use form N92 from the court office. There will be a court hearing with all your creditors. When the court has looked at your circumstances, finances and the offer to repay that you have made, it may agree to pay off the debt. You then repay a fixed amount to the court each month.

Northern Ireland. Here the court system is similar to England and Wales, but the Enforcement of Judgement Office will decide how much you pay.

Scotland. Here the Sheriff Court will hear the case and the procedure will depend on the amount involved.

If your debt is up to £1,000 you will go through the Summary Cause Procedure. You, as 'Defender', will receive a Service Document stating the debt. If you agree the amount but can't pay in full, offer to pay instalments. Fill in Form Q and return it by the set date. If the creditor refuses to accept your offer you must attend court on the Calling Day. Take your financial details and other supporting information.

If you don't keep up the instalments, the Sheriff Officer can order your employer to hold your wages until you agree to have it given to the creditor or he takes action to get it released to him.

If you're out of work the creditor may want to sell some of your possessions (not essentials like clothes, beds, cookers, etc), in which case the Sheriff Officer will call and tell you that you are not allowed to get rid of them. This is known as 'poinding'. They will be sold at a Warrant Sale, and the money will be used to repay the debt. You'll also have to pay the creditor's legal costs against you.

If your debts are over £1,000 you will go through the

Ordinary Cause Procedure. This takes place in the Court of Session in Edinburgh and the process is a little more complicated. It isn't possible at present to pay off debts in instalments.

AVOIDING FINANCIAL SLAVERY

Everyone in financial difficulties dreams of a windfall. With £1,000, £5,000 or £100,000 you could start again with a clean slate. The figure varies from person to person, the hope is the same. It rarely happens, though, and even the lucky few who get such a break often get right back into debt where they started.

The same applies to people who clear their debts the hard way. Why? Because most of us are in financial slavery and have been brought up that way. Society expects it of us!

Bills only arrive because we bought something. Debts arise from a decision to borrow money to pay for something we couldn't afford at the time.

Why did you get into debt? Why did you borrow the money in the first place? Some debts are more sensible than others. Houses are more essential than hi-fi systems. Perhaps something broke and you needed to replace it? Or did you just see the thing and buy it on a whim?

Whenever you read a paper or watch TV you will be told, directly by the advertisers and often indirectly by the images and values portrayed in the programmes, that you ought to have 'things': new, more fashionable clothes, nicer homes, more prestigious cars – all kinds of 'things'. Our family, friends and neighbours often watch the same programmes and expect you to conform to the same images (because if you don't you're saying that they are fools). If you have money to spend, fine. If not? Well, there's always credit. You don't have £1,000 to spend on the gear now? But you can afford £10 a month, can't you? Society (Mammon or the world we talked about in chapter 1) leaves you with two choices: borrow or be rich. The winners in financial slavery are those who can afford to keep up the payments and the appearances. The losers can't and go into debt.

Unless you're rich the only way out of the game is not playing. That takes real courage because most people don't resist and dislike people who do. Society is built on the assumption that wealth is success and buys you anything. Escaping from financial slavery means telling society that it's values are wrong. You may make peace with God in doing so but your 'friends' may declare war on you.

The issue is our real motivation to earn and spend money. Is it important to be seen in the latest fashions, only driving new cars, living in exclusive neighbourhoods, or taking exotic holidays? Most of us care what other people think, but escaping financial slavery depends on understanding whether these things are really important to us and forgetting about other people's idols.

Think again about the rich man in Luke 18: 18–25. He had wealth and status and presumably everything it could buy him. Yet his question to Jesus indicated there was something he wanted which money couldn't buy: 'What must I do to inherit eternal life?' Jesus' reply shocked him: 'Sell everything you have and give to the poor, and you will have treasure in heaven. Then come, follow me.' Jesus makes the point that life's greatest rewards are not financial. They belong in a different league.

Don't get this out of context. The Bible makes it clear that there is nothing wrong with wealth as such. God frequently blesses his followers with it. The rich man's problem was that his *priority* was wealth, hence his sadness at Jesus' reply. Jesus wanted him to get his priorities right.

You don't have to live your life as a slave to the financial system. When fashion designers demand that you line their pockets each season to buy a new wardrobe you have the right to say no. No law says you must drive a brand new car. If a million sheep take three hops and a bounce and go 'Baa', do *you* have to?

What are the things in life that matter to you? Is there something which means more to you than hearing your CDs played on an even more expensive hi-fi? It's the same music. Not everything you find appealing has to involve you in financial slavery. For example, spending time with your children is (usually!) cheap. They can be very entertaining

'Lucky chap – owes nothing!'

and will probably love you for it. If you haven't got your own there are thousands of other people's children in dire straits (many of them victims of their parent's financial slavery). Try joining an organization to help them. Whether you're a Christian or not there are plenty of alternatives to financial slavery, if you've got the courage to get off the drug Mammon.

And here's the really good news. When the prodigal son (Luke 15:11–32) was homeless, broke and starving on the street, the important thing was his turning away from financial slavery and back to his father. He didn't even get home before his father had come running to greet him. God is the same, which is why Jesus told the story. He's not waiting until we're good enough. Our past record doesn't matter. He's waiting for that turning process to begin. God will act in your life, including your finances, as soon as you let him.

Dare to think dangerously and you'll probably find God waiting there for you!

Chapter Six

GETTING IMPARTIAL ADVICE

Kate Price collapsed onto the sofa with a sigh of relief as her husband Donald closed the door firmly behind the insurance salesman. She looked at the clock to discover that the evening news had finished. Now she would have to wait until tomorrow to find out the football scores.

'Have we missed the news?' asked Donald as he came into the room.

''Fraid so.'

'I told you when he phoned you shouldn't have let him visit us. I was beginning to think he'd taken root!'

'He was getting a bit desperate to sell us something, wasn't he? Any chance of a nightcap?'

'Great minds think alike,' smiled Donald, already fishing in the cupboard for a suitable bottle. 'He was a nice enough chap, but what sort of experience do you get in six weeks as a "financial consultant"? What was he before?'

'A building labourer, I think he said.'

'Speaks volumes, doesn't it?'

Kate flicked through the papers the visitor had left them. 'The questionnaire was an eye-opener though, wasn't it? Oh lovely, thanks.' She took the glass he had offered her, took a sip and returned to the papers. Donald settled into an armchair opposite and placed his glass on the table beside him.

'You're not seriously suggesting we buy an insurance policy from him, are you?'

'I'm suggesting that the questionnaire pointed out a few things that I think we should look at, that's all.'

'Like what?'

'Like how I would cope with the kids if you died. Like how would you cope with the kids if I died. There's no way you could afford to keep working and look after them, is there? They hardly see you as it is.'

Roger reflected for a few moments. 'Fair point. But I'm not happy about trusting the family to the financial expertise of a former labourer, are you?'

ENTERING THE FINANCIAL JUNGLE

Most people's first encounter with the financial services industry will be through collective investments like life policies and unit trusts. It may be through buying their first house or as a result of a visit from a salesman. This chapter aims to explain in outline how the business operates, and how to find the right advice and products for you. Let us set the scene, though, with a little fictional nightmare!

Imagine that qualified doctors don't have a near monopoly on the provision of medical advice. Subject only to passing a simple licensing examination, set by drug companies, anyone can sell medicines direct to the public. As the company's agent in law the salesman must promote the interests of the drug company, not necessarily the patient. While he must sell a patient the most suitable drug made by his firm, he is not legally required to refer a patient to another company who have made a better or more suitable drug. He is probably licensed to sell only one or two drugs from the company range because, like most of his colleagues, he will have only been in the business for a few months and hasn't had time to do all the relevant exams. Paid only if he sells, he cannot really afford to sell you nothing. So, rather than refer you to someone who can provide the most suitable drug for your condition, he is tempted (and probably trained, though the drug companies would probably deny it) to make his drug fit your need.

Of course, there are independent practitioners who, as your agent, are legally required to provide you with the most suitable treatment available. They work for you, not the drug companies, and you can sue them if something goes wrong. But unless they actually steal your money, there's little anyone can prove against them. The regulators who enforce the legislation protecting patients are mainly concerned to ensure that the practitioner's stationery is correctly worded, that the paperwork and files have been properly maintained, that the practice is solvent and the accounts have been properly kept, because the actual quality of advice is hard to quantify.

Fortunately medical services have not been organized like this in Britain since earlier times when barbers pulled teeth and charlatans sold potions curing everything from warts to smallpox!

However, professional practitioners might recognize an uncomfortable number of similarities between the above situation and the financial services industry. Are you surprised that the financial health of the average British family is appalling?

There is one obvious way to protect the public from bad, sometimes criminal, advice, which is used by other recognized professions in Britain. To be a doctor, for example, you must be trained and pass some formidable exams. The qualification is recognized by the public, and doctors' behaviour is controlled by a professional body. Restricting practice to properly qualified doctors guarantees them status, respect, and a good income. They can afford and are required to do the best for their patients.

There are two types of financial advisors. Company salesmen work for the suppliers of specific products. As agents they are required in law to further their company's interest. Asking such an agent for independent advice is like asking a motor agent to sell you the best car on the market. He will normally recommend whichever manufacturer pays his wages. The other type are agents for their clients and are required to protect their clients' interests. When you see an agent, make sure you know who he's working for, you or his company, since it may greatly affect the advice you get and the products you are offered. Obviously independent advice will be preferable, but how do you tell the good independent financial advisor (IFA) from the bad?

'I think God just said 'No' to the Sun Policy.'

You can, of course, do all the research and product selection yourself. There is nothing to stop you finding out all the information that an IFA can, since it should all be public knowledge, but to find much of it you need to know where to look and who to ask so, for all but the simplest products, it's usually quicker and more cost-effective to hire someone with the specialist knowledge and expertise in applying it.

The problem with even independent advisors is that good advice is often unmeasurable and the advisors often unqualified. This situation is beginning to change as increasing numbers of courses and qualifications are becoming available.

The business is also still predominantly commission-led and the advice is consequently restricted to products which pay commission. Not unnaturally, since he wants his family to eat too, an independent salesman may give you a better product than a tied agent, but, he may be reluctant to recommend a non-commission product, even though he is legally required to do so.

Part of this problem is with the public. While they remain largely unwilling to pay for impartial advice it will remain largely unavailable. This would probably change if the public realized that frequently they pay at least as much in commission as they would in fees. The disadvantage with paying a fee is that if you stop a plan or policy you're unlikely to get your money back. If the advisor is receiving commission, however, he'll lose a proportionate amount of commission because you won't have paid it to the company.

Increasingly financial advisors are encouraging fee-paying work and largely this is to the client's benefit. Commissions are often handed to the client or invested in the plan itself, enhancing the benefits. Since the commission paid will frequently cover any fees it's a sensible arrangement.

Let us look at some factors to consider when trying to identify the genuinely impartial advisor.

Size

Big institutions like high street banks and building societies are often less likely to collapse than small practitioners. If you use an advisor as an intermediary and only pay money to the actual investment company through the broker, it shouldn't matter if the broker goes bust. Problems occur when small companies take your money into their own in-house funds and then go bust.

Most banks and building societies are tied agents, frequently of their own insurance companies. If you would like to deal with such a firm, go to one of the few that are still independent. Size isn't necessarily a guarantee of better product selections and there seem to be just as many complaints about the way some of the big firms handle investments.

Authorization

To avoid the threat of statutory regulation, the financial services industry has agreed to a series of self-regulatory measures, although there is constant speculation about whether externally enforced regulation would be better. Make sure that the advisor has been properly authorized by the relevant Self Regulatory Organisation (SRO). The SRO's are, of course, types of trade associations, and ever since the 1986 Financial Services Act became law there have been debates about the future of individual SROs. The Securities and Investments Board (SIB) is in overall control and may well authorize different organisations for different sectors of the market in the future. Independent brokers selling retail products like insurance policies and unit trusts are authorized by the Financial Intermediaries, Managers and Brokers Regulatory Association (FIMBRA) or, usually for larger scale portfolio management, the Investment Managers Regulatory Organization (IMRO). Accountants, solicitors and insurance brokers are usually authorized by their own professional body (the Institute of Chartered Accountants, Law Society etc) so long as they only advise part-time. Full-time financial divisions of such firms will be authorized by the main regulators. Salesmen working for insurance companies, by comparison, are authorized by the Life Assurance and Unit Trust Regulatory Organisation (LAUTRO). At the time of writing discussions continue about a merger of LAUTRO and FIMBRA.

Fees

Free advice doesn't exist. Even those insurance companies who claim to offer non-commission paying policies still pay their salesmen by charging you. It's unreasonable to expect anyone to work for nothing and salesmen will inevitably restrict their advice to commission-paying products (even though it's unlawful for an independent advisor to do so) unless you come to another arrangement. The more ethical advisors will encourage you to remunerate them through either commission or a fee. Where practical, opt for the latter. You can agree either a sensible fee for the job, or an hourly rate if you prefer. Commissions will often cover the fees, alternatively ask the broker to enhance the benefits of the policy either by lower plan charges or increased investment. Fees mean that the advisor can offer a non-commission paying product where appropriate without risking bankruptcy.

Qualifications

Until such time as there are compulsory qualifications in the business you will have to trust your instincts. Many experienced and ethical practitioners have no qualifications at all, although some have taken the trouble to pass some exams. The most useful qualifications at present are those offered by the Chartered Insurance Institute (CII), whose Associate and Fellowship courses teach a considerable amount of relevant knowledge. Institute qualified advisors are recognized by the letters ACII and FCII. In addition the CII offers a Certificate in Financial Planning. The Life Insurance Association (LIA) offer Associates (ALIA) and Fellows (FLIA) qualifications which, though not yet as prestigious as the CII's, are relevant and a laudable move by the business to be more professional.

While most people's affairs are not complicated enough to need an accountant, they can be useful for detailed tax planning or even just doing a tax return properly. Chartered and Certified Accountants are recognised by FCA/ACA and FCCA/ACCA respectively.

Recommendations

The experience of people you trust can be useful here. If one of your friends has extensive experience as a client of a particular firm then your search may well be quick and painless. An ethical practitioner knows how difficult it is to find good advice and should not be offended if you ask for a few references. Try to get names of clients who are not his best friends. If you feel strange about doing this, remember that you're employing him to work for you and most employers take up references.

On the principle of seeking the counsel of the wise, it would be nice to be able to recommend Christian advisors because of their beliefs. Unfortunately incompetence seems just as prevalent among Christians in the business, but a technically able Christian financial planner who really does practice Christian ethics is worth finding. There are some around.

Integrated advice from professionals

Some firms, especially accountants and solicitors, are authorized by their own professional bodies to advise on financial services. Those that have established full-time financial services divisions will be FIMBRA authorized. They should have the expertise to provide a complete tax and accounting service, as well as the ability to recommend the best financial products on the market. They will be able to accept fees and may even insist on it.

Because the cost of setting up ard running a financial services division is quite high, many reputable solicitors and accountants, being busy and expensive, often prefer to avoid any personal involvement with financial services and instead refer clients to trustworthy IFAs. This means that the client should get a well-integrated package. Do avoid firms which dabble in financial services on the side. The research required to do it well precludes part-timers. Qualified accountants and solicitors who have become full-time financial planners, though, tend to be very good.

When you've found your IFA watch out for the following:

Advisors must ask for all relevant information about you before recommending anything. They should provide a report summarizing your requirements then giving their recommendations.

Are you being asked to part with your money quickly to benefit from a good opportunity? If so, get a second opinion.

Does the investment rely on tax loopholes? If so, beware. Such loopholes can close quite quickly.

What sort of claims are being made for a product? Apart from company sales literature, is there any independent evidence such as independent surveys or audited financial statements to back such claims?

What is the level of risk involved? Can you afford to lose all your investment?

If you change your mind how fast can you get the money back?

Do you have to pay fees up front? Don't – without good reason. For a long and complicated job try a deposit and staged payments.

Is taking out a policy a condition for something else? If so, go elsewhere.

Make sure you get the advisor's 'terms of business' and the relevant 'Buyers Guide' published by the SRO. Agree with the advisor, preferably in writing, what he is going to do and how he will be remunerated for his work.

Finally, if there is anything you don't understand either about the product or the terms of doing business with the advisor, ask for clarification. If he really can't explain things, consider going elsewhere.

When considering the advisor's recommendation remember that rewards tend to come from equivalent risk. High risk investments are not necessarily bad, but your investments must be at a level of risk you can accept. You have to go to bed every night and it's a good idea if you can sleep too. If you're going to be worried into insomnia, accept slower steadier gains.

There is usually no such a thing as a guaranteed high return investment. If it sounds too good to be true it probably is. If in doubt, stay out. You might be surprised to hear that God will frequently help here. Many people have found that certain investments feel wrong and, by going ahead anyway, have found out why! This book has constantly recommended staying in touch with God on financial matters. Submit such decisions to his guidance and he will make his thoughts abundantly clear.

Chapter Seven

INSURANCE

Mary Bryce was enjoying her new car. Now Neil had a company car they had agreed the one they owned would be her choice. The little compact could have been purpose built for her. The child seats fitted nicely into the back, the boot was just big enough for the weekly shopping, yet 'Robin' (so called because of the colour) was small enough to squeeze into tiny spaces. Robin's like Neil, she had joked to her friends the other day: super nippy and wonderful to handle. Her only possible complaint was the proximity of the children to her ears when they shrieked at each other.

She dropped the car into third and slid round a long bend into her own road, throttle on, no brakes. The two youngsters squealed skidding-tyre impersonations as the G-force pushed them sideways into their seat harnesses. As she straightened the car up they cheered and laughed.

There were few other cars parked in the road so Mary immediately noticed the police car about a hundred yards ahead, about where her own house was. As she slowed down moments later and turned into her own drive, a policeman and woman climbed out and, having straightened their tunics and put on their caps, followed her up the drive.

As she got out of the car she noticed their troubled expressions.

'Mrs Mary Bryce?' the young woman asked.

Realization caused her stomach to churn suddenly and she put a hand on Robin's roof for support. She'd seen this on TV. The police always send a WPC when they have bad news for a wife . . .

WHY DO YOU NEED INSURANCE?

When the sun shines in life there is a great temptation to think that it never rains. People who make proper provision for life's bad times are consequently rare. Protection against sudden disaster is frequently provided by employers as part of a remuneration package or not at all. Christians themselves often dismiss financial protection as a lack of trust in God and accumulating money as indicative of greed and avarice. On the other hand, some people want excessive financial protection, perhaps equating godliness with financial security and prosperity. The sensible way forward often lies somewhere in the middle.

Accumulating surplus for hard times is a sound principle in the Bible. 'Go to the ant, you sluggard; consider its ways and be wise! It has no commander, no overseer or ruler, yet it stores its provisions in summer and gathers its food at harvest' (Proverbs 6:6–8). Problems only arise when excessive hoarding verges on greed, as the parable of the rich fool makes clear (Luke 12:13–21).

Insurance is not specifically mentioned in the Bible, but it should be regarded as a form of storing for bad times. To assume that God will exempt Christians from bad times is presumptuous, ignores reality, and part of providing for a family is preventing a financial disaster from following a physical one. By surrendering a proportion of income (perhaps the only asset one has for much of life) provision can be made against calamity. Paul wrote to Timothy: 'If anyone does not provide for his relatives, and especially for his immediate family, he has denied the faith and is worse than an unbeliever' (1 Timothy 5:8).

Remember that these provisions also apply if you are single as well as to married people. When you die you will have outstanding bills (eg electricity, gas). Will your parents be able to afford to pay them while probate (see chapter 11) is being granted?

Let us look at the two types of provision. Saving, which is a process of storing wealth for future use, will be covered in chapter 10. This chapter will look at insurance which provides money if it's needed before enough can be saved.

INSURANCE AND ASSURANCE

'Insurance' provides money against risks like accidents, fires and other events which may never happen. 'Assurance' provides cover against certainties, like death. In an ideal Christian society both might be unnecessary, since other believers would rally round, meeting the needs of a family in trouble (2 Corinthians 8:13–15). Since our society isn't Christian, insurance companies often provide the best alternative means of mutual support.

WHICH RISKS AND HOW MUCH COVER?

Unless you lose a major capital item like your house you probably won't be left destitute, but it can be annoying and inconvenient to have your clothes ruined or a camera stolen. Your work/ministry may well be affected too. Some of the more minor risks are listed in Table 7.1. If your circumstances dictate, an insurance broker with expertise on 'personal lines' will be able to advise which items can be covered and by whom, although many minor items will be covered by a single household policy. We will concentrate on providing for events that can cause financial devastation.

General insurance

The most important general insurance is probably household insurance covering your home and its contents against damage or loss.

TABLE 7.1 MINOR RISK CHECKLIST

GENERAL INSURANCE

Item	Replacement cost	Present cover
House buildings		
Household contents		
Possessions that leave the home ('All Risks')		

High value items:

Cars		
Works of art		
Computers		
Musical instruments		
Other		

OTHER GENERAL RISKS

	Cover level		
	Necessary	Actual	Shortfall
Third party liability			
Legal expenses			
Other			

If you are a tenant or leaseholder, buildings cover will normally be provided by the landlord (at your expense). Normally this will be taken out of the rent, unless you've bought the leasehold in which case it will be a separate item. In either case you will probably need additional insurance for your home's contents.

If you buy the property, it is unlikely you will be able to complete the purchase without taking out a policy unless you buy for cash. Your mortgage lender will probably try to sell you a policy or, if you arrange your own, charge you a fee for checking it.

Buildings cover should at least pay the costs of repairing or replacing your home in the event of damage or destruction. It should have a mechanism for regularly adjusting that cover to account for fluctuations in house prices and building costs.

The contents part, as the name suggests, covers items in your home. A useful add-on to consider is all-risks insurance, so that items which frequently leave the home are insured when they are off the premises. A good policy will replace damaged items on a 'new for old' basis, where the insurer pays the replacement cost rather the actual value which, for most items, will have reduced since you originally bought the item. Companies often cover additional risks in such household policies, such as third party liability cover, which is almost essential in case someone else is injured, by a tile falling off your roof, for example, and you're liable. People are increasingly inclined to sue these days and settlement sums seem to be going up.

The cost of litigation itself means that people on modest means are rarely able to pursue claims through the courts, since they cannot risk the cost of failure, even where the cause is just. Legal expenses insurance can often solve this problem.

Accident cover could be useful too, especially for frequent travellers. Private medical insurance is controversial. Some rich people feel positively virtuous about using the Health Service and making others pay for their medical care, even if they can afford to contribute to the NHS financially and pay for their own treatment.

Income protection

Most people have one major income-producing asset: their work. Losing the ability to work is often devastating. There are two potential problems:

Loss of income due to death. This is not a problem for the person who dies. Mortality statistics show that nearly a third of thirty year olds won't see their sixty-fifth birthday, and any problems caused by premature death will be solved or suffered by their dependants. Proper life assurance cover will usually prevent a family tragedy becoming a financial one. The cheapest solution is called term cover, but since life assurance can also be an effective way of saving it may be worth using a policy that gives cover and savings. Such policies are called 'whole of life' and their workings are explained in chapter 10.

Loss of income due to illness or disability. This is even more likely than loss due to death. The medical services are very good at saving lives, but their ability to return patients to working fitness sometimes lags behind. Social security figures have shown that thousands of people are unable to work for medical reasons. It is estimated that the odds of being disabled and unable to work for an extended period is four times that of dying before retirement, so insurance cover should be a priority. Apart from an income to maintain food and shelter you may also need alterations to your home to cope with disability, holidays for convalescence and so on. Permanent Health Insurance (PHI) provides an income until you return to work or retire, whichever is soonest. It should not be confused with the much cheaper hospital cover, which pays an income while you are in hospital. That kind of insurance is fine – so long as you recover fast enough to return to work while you are still on the payroll. Some employers, along with the statutory sick pay (SSP) scheme, will maintain your salary for several months. This allows you to elect to defer the start of benefit payments thereby significantly reducing PHI premiums. This form of insurance benefit, when added to any residual income or SSP, can provide up to seventy-five per cent of your previous income.

Critical Illness cover is a form of whole-life cover which

pays out on death or diagnosis of a variety of medical conditions, including some cancers and major organ failures. Along with accident cover it may well be useful in providing a cash lump sum in the event of certain disasters.

The Provision Factfind in Table 7.2 will help you decide how much cover you need to provide in either circumstance. The process is simple. If you are married, work out how much income

'And this is our "Life After Death Policy".'

the surviving members of the family would need in the event of either spouse dying or being unable to work. This should include a non-working spouse. Working out the hourly cost of replacing 'just a housewife' is a salutary experience, and being left with young children and a career isn't the time to find that out.

Then work out how much has already been provided by employers, investments and so on. Be honest about what you've got. You may think your parents will help your spouse and children, thereby saving you a few pounds in premiums. Do your parents agree? Have they got the resources? Is your spouse happy with that arrangement? Likewise, if you are single, what would your relatives need to support you in the event of a long-term sickness or permanent disability?

Once you have worked out whether you have any shortfalls in cover levels you should then see an independent advisor who can arrange the best policies to suit your requirements. The financial services market changes so quickly it is impossible to give advice here on individual policies for specific situations. A good advisor should be up to date on the relative merits of policy types offered by the different companies. He will need three things from you:

1. **The type and amount of cover you want.** Let him advise you on policy type, just tell him what you want it to do.

2. **The amount of money you have available to work with** (see Table 7.3). The chart also asks about saving from surplus income. See chapter 10 for advice on deciding where to invest.

3. **The relative priority** you attach to different covers if you haven't enough to buy everything.

Having looked at the the types of cover, how do the policies the advisor might recommend actually work?

INSURANCE POLICY TYPES

There are only three types of assurance policy, although marketing people make it appear to be thousands. Most of them are 'meetoos': all much the same but differently wrapped.

TABLE 7.2 PROVISION FACTFIND: PERSONAL RISK AND LIFE COVER

	Cover level		
	Necessary	**Actual**	**Shortfall**
Loss of income due to			
1. Illness or injury			
a. Income per year*			
b. Cash on diagnosis**			
2. Death			
a. Mortgage			
b. Other debts			
c. Income replacement***			
3. Medical expenses cover			

* Check with employer for:
    1. Length of time wages/salary will continue, and
    2. Amount of SSP thereafter.

** Only available for certain conditions.

*** Multiply by 10-15 for the cash sum needed assuming 6.7 to 10 per cent per annum return once invested. Subtract existing cash deposits to estimate the cover level required. Consider increasing amount to cover inflation, especially if children are young.

TABLE 7.3 PROVISION BUDGET

Normal monthly/weekly expenditure £

Normal expenditure on:

Essentials

Desirables

Luxuries

Balance available for future provision: £

If balance negative, amount to be diverted from luxuries: £

Amount devoted to provision: £   per month*

PROVISION PRIORITIES
Rank according to importance in your situation

Household and contents insurance

Life cover

Illness and disability cover

Short-term cash savings

Longer-term asset-based savings

Other

In conjuction with your advisor (if any) who can advise on
likely cost, assign an amount to each item until your run out
of available cash, or until each priority is met.

* This questionnaire should be completed in conjunction
with Table 4.1.

Prices vary enormously! There are 'term, endowment and whole of life policies. We'll look at endowments and whole of life in chapter 10 since they are life assurance policies which include investment elements.

Term insurances are all pure protection policies. Basically you agree with the company that if something specific happens (the risk) within a certain period (the term), they'll pay you an agreed amount of money (the sum assured). It might be your death within 20 years, or a car accident within 12 months. For general insurance, illness and disability policies like PHI a good broker is essential. There are plenty of grounds for dispute about precisely what is covered. When and if the event happens you need to be sure that the way it occured doesn't prevent you claiming. (Life assurance is much easier because death is much easier to define.) The simplest policies are level term policies but there are a few variants on the basic model.

Level term insurance

The sum assured remains constant throughout the term. Sometimes these policies come with an 'indexation option' which links the sum assured to rises in either the Retail Prices Index (RPI) or the Average Earnings Index (AEI).

Decreasing term assurance

These are life policies usually used to cover loans, such as repayment mortgages, and are frequently referred to as mortgage protection policies. The sum assured drops at a predetermined rate, intended to match the rate at which the loan is repaid.

Family income benefit

This provides a set income from the point of death to the end of the original policy term. Instead of being paid in a lump sum, the benefits are paid periodically. These are fairly rare today, although they were common during the days when husbands thought their 'little woman' couldn't be trusted with all the money at once. However, this raises a point which is relevant today. It is quite common for one spouse to be solely responsible for the family finances. Could your spouse cope if you are that person? Could you cope if you're not?

Convertible term assurance

Level term insurance which can be converted to any other policy in the company's product range for the same cover level. This sort of policy sometimes comes with renewable options (you can extend the original term), or increase options (another answer to inflation), or a combination of both.

Chapter Eight

BUYING YOUR HOME

Steve Storey sat on his living-room floor surrounded by papers. There were the estate agents' particulars for about a hundred houses, and mortgage brochures from every bank and building society in the high street. Guides from brokers, agents and solicitors, all telling him how to go about buying his new home, mixed with discount offers on everything from DIY goods to patios, double glazing to home electronics. Apparently the only people who didn't have a view on house purchase were his doctor and the dentist. Frankly, Steve was confused.

Why had he decided to buy? He was far from convinced by the popular myth that property prices only go up. A house price collapse had destroyed that illusion. But with property priced at more realistic levels, he rationalized, it should make sense. The likelihood was that, over the long term, he would end up owning an asset without having paid out more than he would have done renting something equivalent.

It would be more hassle to run than just ringing up the landlord if something broke, but worth it for the freedom. He was definitely staying in the area for a few years, so the extra costs of buying were worth paying. Even if he didn't end up making a fortune owning a house, the rent he was paying certainly wasn't coming back to him either.

An afternoon talking to people about mortgages had convinced him that he was playing a sharp market. He had, out of caution, saved nearly a fifth of the price, although he reckoned a tenth should have been reasonably safe. Going in with a deposit that size meant they treated him like royalty. If he'd only had a tenner for everyone who said they had the best deal, he reflected, he wouldn't need a mortgage.

'Oh, to hell with it,' he said. He picked up his phone and called Peter Japlin, church treasurer and financial advisor.

'Peter? Steve Storey . . . Listen, can you do mortgages?'

MOVING HOUSE

Moving house is one of the most traumatic experiences that modern life has to offer, especially if you're buying and selling. Psychologists have even equated the stress levels with losing a close relative. The reason is obvious. Several parties are involved: buyers, sellers, agents, lawyers and often lenders and brokers, and most of them are strangers. There is also a great deal of money at stake and everyone is trying to come out of the deal ahead. Individual interests are not always compatible, so you will frequently have to preside over a morass of conflicting information. Everyone tries to convince you that your aim (to get the home you want) coincides with theirs (to earn a living). You will probably find it cost-effective to hire some specialist help. The trick is to hire people who have a financial interest in giving you the best service possible. The mortgage business is no charity.

MORTGAGES

How much can you afford?

Some people will be in the happy situation of being able to buy a house for cash. If, however, the house you need costs more than you can afford, you will need a mortgage. For the following reasons, you should arrange your mortgage **before** you make an offer on a property.

You know how much you can afford to spend. Estate agents will tend to show you the most expensive properties they can. By knowing your limit you can avoid being tempted to overstretch yourself and risk problems if interest rates rise afterwards.

You can move quicker. This may mean you can negotiate a better price.

Mortgages rely on referees. This means people like employers, who may have more pressing demands on their time than writing references for you. If you need to move quickly, one source of delay is eliminated if the references are already done.

You will have time to find the right mortgage. With hundreds of lenders, most offering several types of mortgage, often at different rates, all mortgages aren't the same.

Do it yourself, or broking?

There is no law forcing you to seek or take advice about which mortgage you should have. You are perfectly free to visit any and every lender in the country to see what they have to offer. It's your time and expense. There are a few short cuts. Mortgage magazines will compare rates, express opinions about the various products and are a useful guide, but remember that journalists are rarely more expert in the matter than you and aren't exactly renowned for factual accuracy. Check all facts given with the lender itself.

If you're too busy to visit every lender, the alternative is to use a financial advisor who offers a mortgage broking service. Read chapter 6 on finding impartial advice. His market knowledge should also include lenders who don't have high street shops, like merchant banks and centralized lenders. Make sure the advisor spends a good deal of his time on mortgages and is not just doing a few on the side. He should have access to at least one computerized mortgage database.

As with any advisor, make sure you both agree how he'll be paid and remember that you may not get impartial advice if he's limited to commission-bearing products.

Types of mortgages

There are basically two types of mortgage: Repayment (or capital and interest); and interest only. The latter can come in a variety of guises.

Repayment mortgages
Your monthly payment includes interest and some repayment of the capital. At the end of the term you will have paid off your loan in full. You will need a mortgage protection policy, usually a decreasing term assurance policy, so the loan is repaid if you die prematurely. The advantages of this type of mortgage are:

1. You will owe nothing at the end of the period.

2. You can usually extend the term of the loan if interest rates rise, keeping your payments level.

3. They tend to be cheaper (lower monthly cost) when interest rates are high.

Interest only
You only pay interest each month, repaying the loan in full at the end of the term. Traditionally the capital sum is saved by using a low-cost endowment policy as the repayment vehicle. Pensions, Personal Equity Plans (PEPs) and unit trust savings plans are also becoming quite widely used. Interest-only loans have the following advantages:

1. The growth assumptions acceptable to the lenders tend to be so conservative that the repayment vehicle may over-fund. This gives rise to the much-loved 'tax-free cash' or its alternative, an early repayment.

2. The value of the saving plan can move house with you, continuing to build up, instead of you having to return to the start of another, say, 25 year loan each time you move. Most people move house a couple of times. By topping up the savings plan if necessary it is still possible to pay off the loan within the original mortgage term. Even if you can't afford the extra contribution rate needed for a short-term top-up policy and take out a 25-year loan anyway, the over-funding built into the policies may still allow you to repay early.

Do not cancel existing plans to start new ones. It's usually unnecessary, rarely in your interest and you pay extra commission.

3. Inflation may erode the value of the loan in real terms by the time you repay it.

4. Basic rate tax relief is available on the first £30,000 of the loan. When the outstanding balance of a repayment loan falls below that amount, the value of that tax relief obviously falls with it.

5. Interest-only loans tend to be cheaper than repayment loans when interest rates are lower.

Journalists seem to prefer loans which reflect interest rate levels and the consequent monthly payment levels prevailing when they write their articles. They tend to prefer the cheapest at the time and some seem unable to consider value for money, forgetting that if their preference changes next year yours probably can't. On the whole interest-only loans can be better value for money in the long term. There is, however, less control over the monthly repayments and you need to be able to withstand higher payments if rates rise.

There is also no guarantee that a savings plan will be able to repay the loan. That depends on the investment success of the institution concerned, although some companies guarantee to repay the loan if you agree to increase the premiums (if necessary) at pre-set review dates. However, if the world economy was doing so badly for so long that all insurance and pension policies, backed by a wide spread of investments, were seriously under-funded there might be more important things to worry about anyway! The more volatile PEPs and unit trusts plans are the most risky, since these are almost entirely equity-based. Even so, stock markets have proven, historically, to be good long term investments.

If you have an interest-only mortgage, for safety's sake monitor your repayment vehicle to ensure it is generating the right result. The old method of calculating with-profit endowment premium rates, for example, used existing bonus rates extrapolated forward. If rates were high when the policy started, as in the early eighties for instance, the premium charged assumed high rates would continue. If subsequent earnings are not high enough the policy could underfund. If your policy has a built in review procedure (most unit-linked endowments have, for example) then any problems will become apparent anyway.

With-profit policies rarely have such a mechanism. Every few years ask the insurance company for an Estimated Maturity Value (EMV). Reversionary bonuses once added to the policy are guaranteed. Terminal bonus is calculated on maturity and depends on earnings experience over the policy term. If the EMV based on reversionary bonus alone exceeds the loan liability the policy is on course. The first danger sign is when the policy relies on terminals to make up a shortfall. If the EMV falls short even with terminals taken into account, then you may have a difference to make up when you repay the loan.

Unless you already have some spare cash the only real solution is to make extra provision. You could save some money using the various savings media described in chapter 10. Alternatively, if you believe investment conditions are poor, for instance, you could make some early mortgage repayments.

Similar principles apply to all repayment vehicles. You should regularly check to ensure the rate of growth is sufficient to cover any expectations you have and take remedial action if needed. An independent advisor should be able to help the review process if the investment managers try to confuse you.

LOAN REPAYMENT VEHICLES

How do the various repayment vehicles work? Life assurance policies which pay out when the loan becomes due are very common. You can use non-profit, with-profit, or unit-linked policies, as described in chapter 10. Buying a full endowment with a sum assured equal to the loan is very expensive. Although the death benefit will equal the loan throughout, the payout will far exceed the loan. Alternatively you can use pensions, unit trusts or PEPs.

Low-cost endowments

These are designed for house purchase and make the monthly payments equate to the cost of a repayment mortgage. The insurance company estimates the sum assured which, given an assumed rate of bonus addition the lender agrees with, will grow to equal the loan at maturity. By including in the policy a term insurance which decreases as the policy value grows, a Guaranteed Minimum Death Benefit (GMDB) is produced in addition well as the sum assured. The company pays the greater of the GMDB or the policy value if the policyholder dies prematurely. The loan should equal the GMDB.

Unit-linked low-cost endowments are combinations of term assurance and unit-linked life assurance savings plans.

Pension plans

Instead of using an insurance policy it is possible to use a personal pension which will produce a fund payable from your fiftieth birthday. Twenty-five per cent of that fund can be taken in cash which can be used to repay the loan. The advantage to you is that you receive tax relief on payments into the plan, which in effect amounts to tax relief on the capital cost of buying the house as well as the interest.

The disadvantage is that you will reduce the pension available to you in retirement. Most people already have inadequate provision for retirement anyway, so pension mortgages have worrying aspects. You should ensure your retirement is secure before even considering using pensions to repay a loan. If you then find yourself selecting a retirement planning route in which the pension you select can be used for mortgage purposes, then you can consider a pension mortgage if you're already making adequate savings elsewhere. Take professional and impartial advice, and don't let anyone construct your retirement planning around his desire to sell you a pension mortgage.

You will need to take out pension term assurance to cover the loan in case you die before retirement and while the pension fund is smaller than the loan. This is also tax deductible.

Unit trusts and PEPS

These are the most recent innovations in the market. They are plans which combine a unit trust savings plan with a term assurance element. They tend to be a little cheaper than endowments, not least because the charging structure rarely meets as heavy a commission element as most endowments or pensions. Both of these vehicles require life assurance, either separately set up or built into the plan, which reduces that advantage.

Being almost totally equity-based, instead of spread across a wide range of assets like most insurance policies, they are more volatile and subject to the fluctuations of equity markets. In the case of a PEP they will largely be tied to the success of EC stock markets. In good years these plans may perform better than an insurance policy, in bad years they may do worse. PEP's also have the tax advantages mentioned in chapter 6.

THE PROCESS OF HOUSEBUYING

First you need to make an initial assessment of your requirements.

Step 1: Where should the house be?

Write down what you want. These are the sort of questions to consider. Where do you want to live? What church will you join and how can you contribute to the community? What is public transport like? Can you park your car? Get a map and look at the access routes. What sort of facilities are there? Where will you shop? What are the schools like? Is there a decent pub? Are there sport and leisure facilities? The relative importance of these things is your decision.

Step 2: What sort of property?

Stay open-minded. Concentrate on number and size of rooms, whether a garden is vital, and how much renovation you are prepared to do or can afford to have done for you. New houses tend to be more expensive to buy but cheaper to run.

Step 3: How much can you afford?

That depends on the amount of money you have saved plus any mortgage you get. At this stage you need to know that lenders will offer you two and a half to three times your regular income. If you are buying with a partner the maximum is likely to be two and a half times your joint income or three times the biggest plus the smallest. These multiples can be exceeded in some cases but you may have difficulty paying later, especially if interest rates rise. Consider taking impartial financial advice on the type and cost of mortgages available.

Househunting

Visit estate agents in the locality you want to move to and see what's available in your price range. They should have considerable local knowledge, but don't let them waste your time with properties that are totally unsuitable or too expensive for you. They may try to sell you a property at the top of your price range because they're acting for the vendors (the people selling the property) and they are being paid on a commission basis, so it is in their interest to get the biggest price possible. The more you pay, the greater commission they receive.

Agents are also famous for 'hype', although recent legislation has tightened up on gushing prose in the property details. Perhaps the only thing unlikely to be described as 'luxurious' is a garage, so make sure you read descriptions of a property quite critically.

Local newspapers and freesheets often have a good selection of property advertisments, usually from estate agents so you will soon get a good idea of price levels in the area. Then find the private adverts. If a vendor can avoid paying an estate agent's fee (about two and a half per cent of the price) they may be more negotiable.

'No need to look further – I like it already!'

Use the Houseviewing Checklist at the end of this chapter whenever you view a property. Don't dismiss a property just because you don't like the decor, but don't be fooled by a slick paint job that may hide a host of faults. Concentrate on the structure and make notes of anything which needs repair. Ask about the cost of running the place and whether you can see recent bills. This includes gas, electricity, and maintenance and repair bills. Ask to see any invoices for recent work and any guarantees still current. Finally, make sure you note exactly what is included in the purchase price. If you're serious about a property, think up some more questions and come back a second time.

Making an offer

The 'asking' price is what the vendor hopes to get. Before making your offer work out roughly how much it will cost to put right the defects you've noted. Then decide how much the property is worth to you and make your offer to the vendor, via the agent if one is involved. You will now need to complete your mortgage application if you haven't already done so, and instruct a surveyor.

Surveys

The minimum you will require is a valuation of the property for the mortgage lender. You will have to pay for this. The surveyor must be acceptable to the lender and they would normally expect you to use a chartered surveyor. Although the valuation will make some reference to the condition of the property, it is advisable to also have at least a house or flatbuyer's survey (a type of survey designed by the Royal Institution of Chartered Surveyors) carried out for your own information. This is a reasonably detailed survey of the condition of the building. It is less detailed, though, than a structural survey. If you opt for this, tell him about anything which worried you when you viewed the property. The more detailed a survey you ask for, the more it will cost, but the less likely you are to get a nasty surprise later. Talk to a local chartered surveyor for details. The lender will probably be able to arrange for a suitable surveyor to carry out a survey and valuation on the same visit if you wish, which might reduce the total cost.

Conveyancing

This process checks all the legal documentation (like title deeds and leases) to ensure there are no irregularities. Checks are also made with the local authorities and the vendor's conveyancer to ensure there is nothing (like a planned motorway, for instance) that will blight the property's value.

At the time you start househunting seriously you must decide whether or not to hire a solicitor or licenced conveyancer to conduct the legal side of the purchase. There are a number of books available which explain how to convey your own property and a great debate about the desirability of doing so. The accepted wisdom seems to be that while any sensible person can convey a house it it is wiser to instruct a professional. Certainly you should not do it unless you are confident at outset of coping with everything involved. Your time may actually be better spent on other activities (like holding down your job!) and paying someone else to do the legal work. How much is your time worth? Also, mortgage lenders are not always happy about you doing your own conveyancing as professionals make their lives easier.

Finding a good conveyancer is essential. A recommendation from someone you trust is wise, but make sure you get quotes for the work from different firms so you know what it should cost, and then negotiate. Since the solicitors no longer have a monopoly on conveyancing they're a lot more reasonable! Make sure they explain exactly what's involved and all extra costs that will be incurred.

You will probably have to keep in touch with your conveyancer to keep things moving as he'll have several cases running simultaneously. Make sure the mortgage offer gets to him as soon after the survey as possible.

Exchanging contracts

As soon as everything is in order you will be asked to sign the contract. At this point you will pay the deposit. The conveyancer then exchanges contract with the vendor or his conveyancer and both parties (in England and Wales) are committed to the deal.

Completion

A date will be fixed by which time all legal formalities will be tied up. On the day you complete the money and keys are handed over and you are free to move in. There is no legal reason why exchange and completion cannot happen on the same day. Solicitors frequently do exactly that on their own purchases. The usual two to four week delay is largely traditional. If that doesn't suit you, tell your solicitor. Unless you arrange otherwise on completion day the money often moves from you to the conveyancers in the morning and on to the vendor when they come back from lunch. Make sure the timings suit you and the others in the chain, since the estate agents cannot legally release the keys until the money is paid. Don't be scared of the conveyancers. Remember that you're doing the instructing and paying.

HOUSEHUNTER'S VIEWING CHECKLIST

Vendor, name and tel no:
Agent, name, contact name and tel no:

Property address:

Type of property:
No of bedrooms   Receps   Bathrms   WCs   Kitchen   Other
Garages   Garden   Other buildings

Asking price   Date/time of viewing:

EXTERIOR ASSESSMENT
(marks out of ten)

Construction/state of repair   Paint work
Window quality   State of roof
Garden   Walls/fences
Drains & gutters

INTERIOR ASSESSMENT
(marks out of ten)

Overall state of repair   Decorative condition
Walls   Ceilings
Woodwork   Damp signs
Plumbing   Electric wiring
Heating   Insulation
Double glazing   Power points

RUNNING COSTS

Electricity
Gas
Community charge
Water

GUARANTEES AND RECENT WORKS

ITEMS INCLUDED IN THE PRICE

Chapter Nine

RETIREMENT PLANNING

One of the great things about being retired, Peter Pomfrey reflected, as his ball pitched onto the green and spun to a halt, *is that you get time to perfect the ability to drop a ball within ten yards of a flag 200 yards away with a three iron*. He pushed the club back into his bag and wandered across to some bushes where his son-in-law, Ian, was looking for his ball.

'OK?' he asked a shaking bush.

'Yeah,' came a breathless reply, 'lousy lie though. Here goes!'

There was a swish and the crackle of disturbed leaf and twig. An orange ball shot into sight about ten yards from Peter and bounced through the light rough onto the fairway.

'Well done. You're safe, if not much further on.'

'Best I could have hoped for. Thank God for luminous balls,' said Ian emerging from the undergrowth and following Peter's gaze. 'Where did you get to? Good grief! You've been practising.'

'I've got the time, at last. I can play every day if I want to.'

'There must be more to retirement than golf.'

'No doubt,' agreed Peter as they walked over to Ian's ball.

'When I fancy, I might have a look round for something more constructive.'

Ian selected an iron, took a few moments to measure his shot and then played to just short of the green. He hadn't put any backspin on the ball so it ran on, narrowly avoiding the lip of a bunker guarding the green from wayward shots and finished up leaving him a fifteen-foot putt for his par. He looked at Peter and smiled, 'A touch fortunate perhaps.'

'They all count,' said Peter.

'I take it that after years at the bank you've a good pension, then. If you can afford to play a round a day, that is,' Ian observed as they set off towards the green.

'If you can call a thirty per cent pay cut "good", yes.'

'I thought you got a full pension?'

'I did more or less, after nearly forty years service. But full pensions are still a pay cut. Not that it matters. Working in the bank means I've seen enough penniless old people on benefits to know that one needs to plan retirement properly. If you think about it you're hoping to be living on an unearned income for about twenty years. Think how much you'd need tomorrow if you wanted to take twenty years holiday. Just growing old doesn't reduce the cost that much, you know. Quite the reverse sometimes.'

'But you've payed off your mortgage and everything, haven't you?'

'Oh, years ago. Not that it cost much with the bank subsidy. But I still made sure we've got plenty on deposit, as well as a bit of unit trust and some insurance.'

'Aren't you paying a lot of tax then?'

'Never really thought about it, Why?'

'Oh, one of my people was retiring the other day and was telling me about a seminar he went to. They were talking about doing an overview of all his assets so that he could get the maximum spendable income from what he's got. Using the different tax regimes, all that sort of thing.'

Peter considered a moment. 'Now that's not a bad idea, Ian. Do you know who was doing the seminar?'

TIME TO STOP?

Most people believe they will stop working in their sixties partly because society has decided they will, partly because they feel they deserve a rest. In fact, working fifty years at the mill, collecting the clock and spending your sunset years dozing by the cottage fire is a folk tradition existing mainly in advertisements. It isn't necessarily a part of the Christian life. Many active Christians find that they work harder and/or more productively in retirement than they did before. The pension just means their work need not turn a profit.

There is also a much darker reason why that image isn't born out by reality, even among the population as a whole. The government (but, in fact, other taxpayers) is expected to provide retirement incomes; however, most people's expectations are usually well beyond the taxpayer's ability to finance them. Consequently the country is full of old people finding that state pensions don't go far and they've no time to plan an alternative.

If you're not going to work after sixty you effectively have to provide for twenty or thirty years unemployment, perhaps more. Many people don't worry about what they're going to live on until they're almost old enough to retire, by which time it's too late to start gathering the enormous amount of cash needed for a comfortable retirement.

Our society has a number of ways for people to achieve a wealthy retirement. This gives Christians the opportunity to plan a part of their lives in which they can do worthwhile and perhaps non-profit making work without worrying about the next paycheque.

This chapter has two sections. One will explore the options available when planning for retirement, a process which should ideally begin as soon as you start work. The second will look at ways to organize yourself once you give up full-time paying work.

PRE-RETIREMENT PLANNING

Like many things designed by a consensus of conflicting interests, the present system of retirement provision is a confusing attempt to please everyone. Most people now have an opportunity to equip themselves with an adequate income in retirement without vested interests, like employers, threatening their well being. Let us begin by looking at what you'll get if you and your employer do nothing and then look at the various options you have for supplementing your retirement income.

The state pension

This is paid for through National Insurance (NI) contributions which are compulsory unless you're earning very little. It comes in two parts.

State Basic Pension
This is paid to everyone who pays enough contributions. If you're not working you can make voluntary contributions. Many people know this as the 'old age pension'. It is adjusted by the Chancellor of the Exchequer each year to take account of inflation.

State Earnings Related (Additional) Pension (SERPS)
SERPS is available only to employees. Your entitlement will depend on the number of years you have worked, your earnings in those years, and (for those retiring after 6 April 1999) 'home responsibilities protection'. This makes allowances for things like time off to bring up children, etc. The final figure will vary and relates to 'band earnings', those between the NI lower earnings limit (earnings below this don't attract NI charges) and any upper earnings limit (earnings above which neither attract charges nor count for earnings-related pension). Assuming your income is between these levels you might attract an earnings-related pension of perhaps fifteen to seventeen per cent of your salary at retirement, on top of your old age pension. Thereafter additional earnings don't

count. These estimates use the calculation scales that will be introduced for people retiring after 1998 as part of the revision to SERPS intended to make it affordable in the twenty-first century. The NI limits are reset each year in line with inflation and can be obtained from the Department of Social Security (DSS), a professional advisor or company providing pensions.

You may opt out of SERPS if you belong to certain types of company pension schemes (called 'contracting-out schemes'), or if you choose to have part of the SERPS element of your NI contributions paid to your own personal pension scheme.

The most obvious thing that can be said about state pensions is that relying on them could cause you financial problems. You may well find your income dropping overnight by thirty to sixty per cent, assuming you get full SERPS benefits on all your earnings! The taxpayer has never really met old peoples' expectations of living standards. With the proportion of old people in the population rising relative to the work force, it may become harder to persuade fewer workers, all trying to bring up their own families, to divert larger shares of their incomes to pensioners who failed to plan properly. Some form of private provision is likely to be essential.

Providing your own pension

If you prefer not to throw yourself on the taxpayer's mercy there are two sources of money for additional retirement provision: an employer or yourself.

If your employer will not provide any kind of pension arrangement you need a personal pension scheme. These are really simple. You invest money with a 'pension provider' (usually an institution like an insurance or unit trust company). All contributions are tax deductible, so tax relief is added and the whole lot grows, free of tax, until you want to cash it in, anytime you like between fifty and seventy-five. You can have a quarter of the money tax free in cash, the rest buys you a pension for life. Prior to 1987 there were also 'section 226' policies (so named from the Income and Corporate Taxes Act 1970, s 226), available to the self employed or those in employment which offered no occupational scheme. These operate in the same way, but were replaced by personal pensions. However, they have some advantages over personal pensions so, if you have one, try to keep it going. See an impartial advisor who can explain how useful they can be as part of a pension portfolio.

Anyone with any earnings that carry no existing pension rights (including part–time jobs) can have a personal pension and you can invest up to seventeen and a half per cent of those earnings each year (more if you're aged over 35). Unless you're self-employed, basic rate tax relief is paid direct to the plan by the taxman through a system called Pension Interest Relief at Source (PIRAS).

In the future there will be fewer workers and so many pensioners that the country won't be able to afford SERPS at its original level. The government is, therefore, encouraging people to leave the scheme. Money you presently pay into SERPS can then go to a personal pension of your choice. Depending on your age and the growth assumptions used, this can be a better deal, especially for younger men and women. Most advisors will help you work out which way will benefit you best and explain why. As you get older you may also find it worth re-entering SERPS.

If you leave SERPS, remember that the pension fund built up by your rebates is only a replacement to SERPS and will probably be inadequate on it's own. If you want a comfortable retirement consider investing some of your own money in addition.

Wherever the money comes from, your retirement income depends on the fund that has accumulated by your retirement date. There are no guarantees (funds that give guaranteed growth rates are usually from cash investments like building societies, see chapter 10 for historical experience of holding cash long term). Any advisor will be able to illustrate likely benefits at a range of anticipated growth rates, with advice on inflation. You can then adjust the investments as you go along to achieve a proper pension.

Advice on selecting a personal pension provider is given at the end of the chapter.

Employer-funded or occupational schemes

Employers often offer a good deal, especially if you're a long-serving employee working for a large organization. If you're young or job-mobile you may be better off making your own arrangements, because the transfer value when you move may be very low. If you join a company scheme, keep track on your likely benefits to avoid your entitlement giving you a nasty shock on retirement day. All schemes must make available a booklet giving details of the pension scheme and an annual report showing how the pension fund is performing. You are also entitled to an annual benefit statement if you ask for one. This will give you full details of the growth of your pension entitlements within the scheme.

Schemes operated by employers may be designed to supplement SERPS ('contracted-in' or 'participating' schemes) More commonly, especially among large employers, schemes will be 'contracted-out' of SERPS. This means that you pay lower national insurance charges because you will not pay contributions to SERPS. On retirement you will receive only the basic state pension, plus any company pension.

There are two types of employer-sponsored pension schemes, final salary and money purchase. A few employers co-operate in funding their employee's personal pensions.

Final salary

Pensions are based on your salary at retirement and proportionate to your length of service. These schemes are common amongst large employers. Your pension normally accrues at one-sixtieth (sometimes one-eightieth) of final salary per year of scheme membership, to a maximum of two-thirds. Some of the pension can be changed (commuted) to a cash sum. If you leave a final salary scheme you will always receive any of your own contributions. If you leave after less than two years service, the employer isn't required to let you keep any money he may have invested for you. Even if you have worked for two years or more, he may not let you take away more than he has to by law. These plans favour long-serving employees, and are hard to beat if you are going to be with the same employer and/or pension scheme for most or all of your career.

Money purchase

These schemes do not guarantee a particular proportion of your final salary. They are contribution-led like personal pensions. The employer invests money and usually requires you to invest a percentage of your own salary. The fund provides a pension proportionate to the size of fund available at retirement, to a maximum of two thirds of your final salary. You can again commute some of the pension to tax-free cash. These plans are more portable from one job to another, not least because it is easier to establish what the fund is worth when you leave. Check to ensure your employer is putting in a reasonable amount of money each month.

Employer-funded personal pensions

While under no obligation, employers have become more inclined to invest in their employee's personal pensions instead of setting up employer-sponsored schemes. This is particularly prevalent where a small employer is concerned about his employees well-being in retirement but wants to avoid administering a company scheme. If you're job-mobile, especially in young and rapidly changing sectors of the economy, this combines career flexibility with an employer's financial contribution.

If you have a personal pension it's worth inviting your employer to contribute. Many sensible employers are reasonable people who are just too busy to think about employee retirement. Pensions may leap up his list of priorities if his staff start talking about them. Given the shortage of skilled labour, many will prefer to avoid staff leaving to join firms with better provision.

More suspect are 'group personal pensions', sold by some pension providers to employers who would like to claim they're offering pension schemes. There's no guarantee that they will pick good schemes, so if you're offered one take impartial advice about your circumstances and the pension provider. It may well be advisable to go and find a better personal pension plan on the open market, then ask your employer to put any money he may be contributing into your own plan. It won't cost him any more or cause him any extra work, so reasonable employers often agree.

In some cases the employer may only be doing the paper-work for your money and offering none of his own. In this case put your money into the plan of your choice and invite him to contribute on top. He can only say no.

If you do decide it is in your interests to leave an employer's pension scheme, your fund will continue to be invested by the company towards your retirement. This is known as 'preserved rights'. Contributions made since 6 April 1988 may be transferred to your personal pension if you wish. Those made before this date can only be transferred with the agreement of the scheme managers.

Additional voluntary contributions

If your occupational pension is going to be insufficient, or you're unlikely to stay with the firm to retirement but are reluctant to forego the firm's inputs, consider some form of Additional Voluntary Contribution (AVC). You can invest up to fifteen per cent of your salary, less any contributions you're already paying. Contributions, as in all pension plans, are fully tax deductible and can be made either through the employer's scheme, or to a Free-Standing Additional Voluntary Contribution (FSAVC) arrangement with an institution of your choice. Which you choose should depend on your circumstances and the investment options the main scheme provides. FSAVCs allow you to pick from the best pension providers on the market. Your employer may only have two or three different options. These often include a with-profit pension policy with an insurance company, a building society and perhaps a unit-linked fund. Unless you're very close to retirement, or the world's asset markets are in free-fall, the building society is unlikely to be a good long-term bet for reasons already discussed. If the asset-based plans, either unit-linked or with-profit, are with top companies (the sort you would pick on their own merit) then investing through your employer's scheme may well be best, especially if there is some arrangement whereby commission charges built into the policy are reduced and the difference paid into your fund.

In 1989 the government introduced a ceiling on the tax relief available to those joining occupational schemes or setting up new personal pensions after March 1989. Those affected can only receive tax relief on contributions that relate to earnings up to £60,000pa (the base ceiling set in tax year 1989/90). This figure will be raised in line with inflation. In Britain we consistently award ourselves inflation-plus pay rises and the government may use prices rather than wages as the index for increases. Cynics fear they will. This will have the effect, in the long term, of reducing tax relief for everyone, even though this will start with the wealthy.

This may be a factor for those on high enough salaries who are trying to decide whether to opt out of their existing scheme, or who are ceasing contributions to their existing pre-1989 plans. The new limits only apply to those who joined occupational schemes before 14 March 1989, and personal pensions set up with effect from 6 April 1989.

It isn't cheap to provide a big enough fund to keep you for perhaps a quarter of a lifetime. You need to consider carefully the scheme your employer provides before deciding whether or not membership is in your interest. If you're in any doubt take proper impartial advice.

FINANCIAL PLANNING IN RETIREMENT

There are basically two types of retirement: forced retirement due to, say, redundancy or ill-health; and planned retirement in which you give up whatever employment you may have had. The latter is likely to be a less anxious and more comfortable experience. A similar approach should be adopted to financial planning in either circumstance. The following sequence of decisions will help you to organize your resources to support your chosen lifestyle, instead of your lifestyle supporting your finances. Compromises will probably be inevitable, especially in enforced retirement, but let's at least aim for comfort and a level that can be sustained.

Step one: deciding on a lifestyle

Be it a blessing or a curse you will probably have much more time. God may wish you to pursue a particular project.

CHECKLIST 1: RETIREMENT INCOME REVIEWS
A summary of your options for action

IF YOU'RE EMPLOYED BUT NOT IN AN OCCUPATIONAL SCHEME
You could do nothing and receive state pension and any
SERPS you qualify for, or:

1. Join the company scheme if available.

2. Take out a personal pension and remain in SERPS.

3. Take out a personal pension and leave SERPS.

IF YOU'RE SELF-EMPLOYED
You can do nothing and get state pension only (no SERPS for
the self-employed) or take out a personal pension.

**IF YOU'RE IN AN OCCUPATIONAL SCHEME CONTRACTED-IN
TO SERPS**
You may choose:

1. To do nothing.

2. To make AVC payments to your company scheme.

3. To stay in SERPS and take out a FSAVC.

4. To opt out of SERPS using a separate ('NI rebate-only')
Personal Pension or FSAVC to collect the SERPS NI rebates.

5. To leave the company scheme and use a personal
pension but remain in SERPS.

6. To leave the company scheme and SERPS, take out a
personal pension and use it to collect SERPS rebates and
your own investments.

IF YOU'RE IN A CONTRACTED-OUT OCCUPATIONAL SCHEME
You have broadly the same choices as those contracted into
SERPS, except you're already out of SERPS. You would have
the choice of rejoining SERPS if you left the scheme.

IF YOU'RE UNEMPLOYED
You are entitled to any benefits accumulated during periods
of employment, including SERPS. If you're signing on then NI
contributions are being paid on your behalf, earning you
state pension rights. If you are concerned about your pension
rights, contact your local DSS office and ask for a pension
forecast.

CHECKLIST 2: PICKING PENSION PROVIDERS GUIDLINES FOR SELECTING THE RIGHT HOME FOR YOUR MONEY

There are literally hundreds of pension plans to choose from and they all claim to be best! Check for the following.

1. The longer the term between application and retirement date the higher the charges build into the plan, especially with insurance company pension plans. Don't select a retirement date later than is necessary for your circumstances. A good advisor is worth a reasonable commission but better still, agree a fee for his work and put any commission into your pension fund.

2. Consider a 'waiver of premium' option. They cost about two per cent of the contributions but mean the plan still continues if you are disabled before your retire. Otherwise, with no suitable earnings you may have to stop the policy.

3. Does the pension provider have a good, long-term, investment record? It's no guarantee of future performance, but it's not a bad indicator. Can it be substantiated from a range of independent surveys and over significant timescales? Remember that Churchill could have said 'there are lies, damned lies and then statistics' about financial services sales literature.

4. What are the costs of stopping or changing regular contributions? The best schemes are very flexible and shouldn't charge much more than a sensible administration fee.

5. Do you get an 'open market option' when you retire? You must buy an annuity from an insurance company to provide the actual pension. There's no way you can predict which company will be offering the best annuity rates decades ahead. Find the best investment manager you can and ensure the plan lets you buy the annuity elsewhere if required (most will).

6. Make sure you can change your mind over retirement date. You may want to keep working, retire early, or slow down gradually. How much will it cost? The best plans are in segments to make this easier.

You may no longer need to live in Rat Race City and can contemplate a move. So start to look at the following aspects of your lifestyle.

Activity
Are you planning to spend your life playing golf or painting pictures? Is there a job you intend to do? Will it pay? Think about your health, too. Formerly sedentary office workers suddenly over-exerting themselves in the garden are apparently prone to fatal heart attacks!

Location
If you are planning to move it may be best to move early. You may still have contacts, better transport, relative youth, and perhaps more money on your side. You may be in the new home for the rest of your life so you will want time to make new friends. Do remember that you may not get any fitter, so make sure that shops, medical services and the other necessities are accessible.

The new budget
How much of an income will you need to support your chosen lifestyle? Table 10.1 will help you examine your financial resources. These will include private, state and company pensions. Don't forget to ask the Department of Social Security about benefits like income supplements to which you may now be entitled. Have you a capital surplus accumulated? Are there any lump sums likely to arrive in the future, for example, life policies that have still to mature? Once you have listed them all look at chapter 4 on budgeting and in particular Table 4.1.

The second part of the budget is anticipated expenditure. In retirement money should go further. Commuting costs, special work clothes, etc may be unnecessary. Time pressures often increase consumption of convenience foods, which are expensive. All these additional expenses can probably be pruned back. Then there are the perks of old age. In addition to some benefits you may get subsidized transport. There are often discounts for pensioners including entertainment and eating out. One restaurant chain recently offered half-price nights to OAPs and their outlets were full of people who had driven from miles around (many in their brand new cars) to enjoy the subsidy!

Step two: using capital to fund income

Once you have assessed the capital resources at your disposal you can work out how long they will support anticipated expenditure. This is a function of three variables: the income you intend to extract; future growth of the capital; the requirement to increase income to counter inflation.

A number of financial advisors have developed computer models to calculate how long your resources will last. By assuming likely rates of growth, inflation and spending, the computer can show whether you have sufficient resources to achieve your desired lifestyle.

You may find you have not got enough for your plans,

especially in forced retirement situations. This means changing the assumptions. You can tell the advisor to use a more optimistic view of inflation or a higher risk but higher yielding investment. Both have obvious dangers. Alternatively, find ways to cut spending or take up some gainful activity. Reorganizing your assets may improve your tax position and disposable income.

Background considerations for planning decisions

Your tax situation may change sharply on retirement. When you are 65 you may claim a higher personal tax allowance, called 'age allowance'. This applies to all income up to an age-allowance income limit. If you exceed the limit the allowance will be cut back by the excess and you will have to pay extra tax on those earnings. This is called the age allowance trap. The income limit is adjusted each year and is a five-figure sum.

Make best use of tax shelters. Use the assets attracting tax first, leaving for later any still growing in tax shelters, like pension funds. Then top up the accessible savings when they run out. Many people take all their pensions up front and put spare cash in the building society. Both will suffer income tax. If you defer taking the pension (easy with personal pensions, but check with your employer if you've a company scheme) the fund will grow free of taxes (and probably faster than in the building society). Meanwhile the annuity rates (the amount you will eventually get per pound of pension fund) will increase simply because you are getting older.

Use your Capital Gains Tax (CGT) allowance. It gets easier to avoid tax liability in retirement. Certain investments can defer income and/or any tax liability. Others will grow subject to CGT instead. You are permitted several thousands of pounds each year in capital gains, tax free. Organize yourself accordingly. Consider investments in assets like equities, unit and investment trusts, and loan stock. If equities are a bit risky for you, look at loan stock such as stepped preference shares in investment trusts. These pay a pre-determined capital sum after a number of years and a rising income during the term. The capital growth is CGT liable, so you only pay income tax on the income you're taking out.

Don't take more income than necessary. If you've more income than you need, look at life insurance bonds, which defer income tax, and perhaps zero-coupon preference shares in investment trusts. The latter also pay out a pre-determined sum on maturity which is subject to CGT and pay no income (hence the zero-coupon) in the meantime. Spare cash can thus profitably be stored for later.

There are ways to organize your assets to minimize the amount of tax you are liable to pay and achieve the best spend-able income from them. You also need to consider what you want to happen to the cash when you've finished with it.

You may wish to give away money to your children or grandchildren. While you are alive you will probably need control of the assets, but some are easier to give without encumbering the inheritor with a large inheritance tax bill. This subject is too specialized for this book to cover in great detail and professional advice should be sought. Your will should be written in conjunction with such advice and planning may take a number of forms.

Life Assurance Bonds, for instance, are investment vehicles for capital in which income tax payments are deferred until the bond is encashed. On encashment the total gain (selling price minus original value) is divided by the total number of years that the bond has existed or since the last chargeable event (eg a withdrawal). This is called 'top-slicing'. The resulting figure is added to the owner's income that year and taxed at the resulting tax rate. So you pay no tax on a bond's gain in value until you cash it in. This reduces your taxable income in the meantime.

When you wish to give money to, say, a grandchild, the bond is assigned to him. When he takes money the top-slicing still occurs, meaning he's acquired a significant capital sum with virtually no tax liability. If he's not a taxpayer when he encashes it (a student, for instance) he may pay no tax at all. Bonds can be segmented (split into lots of little bonds) to make the whole thing even more flexible if plans change later.

A similar thing happens with an equity or unit trust portfolio which you wish your inheritors to receive after your death. Capital gains that your equities make in your lifetime are liable for CGT and you can make several thousand pounds each year without paying tax. When you die any CGT liability dies with you so the full value of the inheritance passes on, although there may be some inheritance tax to pay depending on the total value of your estate.

There are many such devices that can be used quite legally. Your priority might be making best use of the money now, passing it on later or a combination of both. A good financial advisor will be able to tailor asset distribution to your requirements and will be well worth his fee for doing so.

Remember that dying without a will (intestate) can cause a considerable amount of financial grief to your survivors in addition to their grief at your demise. Some families will treat each other with kindness, consideration and concern for your wishes and survivor's needs. For others, the smell of free money in large quantities will have at least some family members and their solicitors gathering like vultures! Fairness, needs and justice may not be the result of this kind of in-fighting, so make a will. Chapter 11 looks at the process of organizing one's affairs properly.

Inheritance tax (IHT) Contrary to popular belief, this tax affects most families with a house, a decent pension and a couple of good life assurance policies. The tax is levied on the surplus if the assets you leave exceed a certain amount. (This is reviewed each year and is a six-figure sum.) There are certain exemptions, like gifts between spouses or to registered charities, and annual limits for IHT-free giving. Gifts made less than seven years before death will be added back into your estate and taxed on a sliding scale.

Many people quite legitimately take the view that the next generation can worry about its own tax bill. Others may wish to reduce that liability, and asset organization can help achieve this. Alternatively it may be easier to accept the liability and insure the donor. The policy is placed in trust to the inheritors and pays enough to meet the tax bill when the donor dies. If you're insuring your own life in this way, remember that the premiums may be treated as a gift to the inheritors unless they are paid from your normal income. Check the sum assured every year to ensure it still covers the liability.

Detailed IHT planning is also the province of the professional advisor.

Money accumulated prior to retirement may have to sustain you for a quarter of your life, so it makes sense to make proper provision during your working life. When you retire you will probably find that proper organization can make whatever resources you have go considerably further. Good advice from an impartial advisor is essential and will pay for itself many times over.

RETIREMENT RESOURCES SUMMARY

INCOME SOURCES
Basic state pension

SERPS

Social security benefits

Graduated pension (earned
from 1961-1975 only)

Personal or s 226 pension

Company pensions

Working income

Interest from cash deposits

Income from dividends, etc

Other

CAPITAL RECOURCES

Type	Size, income pa and any escalation expected
Equities	
Loan stocks (inc gilts)	
Buildings	
Other	

FUTURE CAPITAL RECOURCES

Type	Date and amount, potential growth, etc
Life policies	
Deferred or Deferrable pensions	
Other (eg inheritances)	

Chapter Ten

SAVINGS AND INVESTMENTS

Robert had asked Peter Japlin, financial advisor and part-time church treasurer, to write a guide to Christian investment. 'The thing I find difficult,' said Peter, is advising clients on investments.'

'But you do it for a living!' said Robert, his eyebrows raised.

'Oh, heathens aren't a problem if they just want to maximize wealth and give as little as possible to the taxman. It's the Christians who say their priorities are different.'

'Does that affect actual investment decisions?' asked Robert.

'Well, most small savers' priority is maximum gains without much risk. I normally advise saving with a bank or building society and perhaps some suitable savings plans. That should give a spread of assets to keep down risk and decent growth because the money is properly managed.'

'And that's a problem?'

'In purely investment terms, no. But your sermons imply we need to look further. "Ethical" investments perhaps? Mind you, it's ironic how many managers throw alcoholic and tobacco-reeking lunches to persuade me how ethical their fund is because it boycotts brewers and tobacconists. Is it parting the conscience-struck from their money or a way to have a genuine effect through investment?'

'Ethical investment is difficult then?'

'It's an intellectual minefield. If we'd boycotted the British arms industries in the thirties, for instance, we might not have had the option of opposing Hitler. As for types of investment, collective funds are good value, but inevitably you have less control. Real influence comes from owning part of the underlying business and making your voice heard at shareholder meetings.'

'I can see why most people stick their money in a building society.'

'But is that a solution? Isn't lending money usury? The Bible is pretty ambivalent about that at the best of times!'

'Certainly God gets upset about oppressive lending practices and charging excessive interest.'

'Is repossessing borrowers' homes oppressive in the Bible's terms? How does that equate with the situation in Nehemiah 5? Lend to a building society and as a member those houses are actually being repossessed on your behalf. So why don't Christians turn up at meetings? When did you last hear of a call to boycott building societies?'

'That's thought provoking, certainly,' agreed Robert. 'So what are you going to put into our guide?'

'Well, I see nothing wrong with investment as such, nor clubbing together to form building societies to lend house purchase money to each other, either. The structures themselves are fine. It's individual behaviour that counts. If I explain how certain popular investments work, the readers can make up their own minds about ethics. If ever there are cases to judge on their merits, individual investments, are they . . .'

FOR A RAINY DAY?

Once our basic spending needs are taken care of and we have protected our family in case disaster strikes, we can look at savings from any surplus income. The selection of the most suitable medium for saving depends on several factors:

1. The level of risk you will accept to try for better returns.

2. The loss, if any, of access you will accept to achieve better returns.

3. The time, expertise and/or desire you have to administer the investment.

4. The cost of making the investment.

It may be helpful to think of money in the following time accessible bands.

First-line reserves

Most savers should start by building up a cash sum on immediate, or at least short-term, access, perhaps a month at most. The profits will not be very high, but such investments are cheap and fairly safe, at least in the short term. Money is separated from the daily spending current accounts and deposited in a bank or building society interest-paying account. Very costly emergencies should probably be covered by insurance, so this fund is intended to cover unforeseen items like breakages or planned major expenses like holidays. As a guide, two or three months' income is about the right amount unless you are saving for a major purchase in the immediate future.

Medium-term reserves

Having achieved a cash surplus for short-term use, some medium-term cash can be stored in less accessible, riskier and perhaps faster growing investments. These include more adventurous savings plans, like unit and investment trusts and life assurance savings policies. These are linked to assets like property and equities (stocks and shares). Such investments should be allowed at least two to three years to cover management costs and overcome market fluctuations before being expected to show better returns than cash deposits. In poor markets though, they make take longer, or even fall in value. One obvious use is education costs but major capital expenditure like a car could be provided this way.

Long-term reserves

These are for expenditure planned in ten or more years time. Immediate access to money is therefore a lower priority than potential growth, cost and tax efficiency. A longer-term view may mean day-to-day or even annual value fluctuations are more acceptable. A wedding is a classic event provided for in this way; retirement money is perhaps the most important long-term priority.

Different financial goals can, therefore, be co-ordinated within such timescales. Different types of investment also have certain characteristics which affect their suitability for different tasks. We will now look at the major savings media that are presently available.

CASH SAVINGS

This is the simplest way of saving. You lend the money to a bank or building society, or to the Government through National Savings, and in return they pay you interest. There are generally no charges, but the returns are not very exciting. Access is good unless you have agreed to give a period of notice in return for higher interest. The short-term risk is slight, since banks, building societies and the British government rarely go bust.

The interest would normally be subject to income tax if your income is high enough, unless you hold it in an offshore account offered by banks and building societies, or in offshore currency funds, operated by some of the financial institutions. In either case the interest would be taxable if you bring the money back onshore.

You should consider having a Tax Exempt Special Savings Account (TESSA) which allows anyone over 18 to save up to £9,000 over a period of 5 years and receive their interest free of tax. You cannot withdraw any capital during the term and still qualify for tax relief, although there are ways to withdraw net (after tax) interest at any time.

The biggest risk in saving cash is that the value of money tends to decline. (This is what is called inflation.) If you spend any interest your capital value is eroded. Even if you re-invest the interest at a lower rate than inflation, the spending power of your money still falls. This has been a problem in recent decades. £1,000 invested, with interest re-invested, in a building society in the mid 1940s was worth less than £500, in real terms by the late 1980s. (This is the real effect of the country living beyond it's means and successive governments printing money to fill the gap.)

ASSET-BASED SAVINGS

Owning real assets, like buildings and businesses, can reduce or even eliminate the effect of inflation. They earn money for their owners (dividends and rents) but as the value of money falls their nominal value rises because it takes more cash to buy them. If other people decide to own them, perhaps because their profitability is likely to increase, their real value rises. Well selected investments, therefore, grow in real value.

Of course the daily price of capital assets fluctuate. This risk element is greater in some markets than others, hence the traditional wisdom of spreading investments. Markets are driven by fear and greed, and when one seriously outweighs the other they will move rapidly up or down. In the 1920s, 1970s and 1980s, stock markets were driven higher by floods of money, but collapsed as investors thought the end of the world was nigh. Most of the time, though, the gains have outweighed losses over the long term and people have generally done much better in assets than cash, largely because of inflation since the Second World War.

The main assets to consider when investing are the following.

Equities

These are shares in companies, usually those traded on the stock exchange. There are various types of share, but broadly speaking the shareholder owns part of the business itself. Personal Equity Plans are a government initiative which allow you to hold European Community (EC) equities (the shares of EC companies traded on the stock market) or predominantly EC-investing unit trusts. Normally you pay income tax on the dividends that shares or trusts pay out, and Capital Gains Tax on any profits you make from buying and selling shares. These taxes do not apply to shares held in a PEP.

Fixed interest securities

These are IOUs issued by businesses and institutions such as local authorities or governments. They are also called 'loan stock'. The safer the loan, the lower the rate of interest or redemption yield. Loans to the British government, for example, (known as gilt-edged stock or gilts because the original records of such stocks were kept in gilt-edged ledgers) would, in theory, only lose the investor his money if the government went broke, so they are considered low risk and pay lower interest. During the mid 1980s, on the other hand, loans to companies in high risk expansion and acquisition programmes were funded by selling securities paying huge interest rates. These were called junk bonds, a name that proved more accurate than many had hoped.

Property

This usually means commercial buildings such as office blocks, shops, factories and farms. Holding residential property as an investment is less common and hardly less risky, despite folklore to the contrary!

These assets pay income subject to income tax. Equities pay dividends, properties earn rents, loan stocks pay interest. If the asset's price increases, a capital gain is caused when they are sold and that gain is subject to Capital Gains Tax (CGT), except for profits from gilts trading which are CGT exempt but potentially liable to income tax.

Assets like futures, minerals and fine art are beyond the

'It's make your mind up time pal! Do you or don't you want to buy some junk bonds?'

scope of this book, but will be mentioned briefly at the end of the chapter.

If you want to invest directly in such assets you will be pitching your skills against people who do it for a living. With quicker access to price sensitive information they are better able to calculate when to buy or sell. They often buy cheaply and, as prices rise, sell to the small investors who are persuaded to enter the market by greed and ill-informed press comment. With no one else to sell to, the latecomers take either 'the long-term view' (City-speak for waiting for prices to return to the peak level you mistakenly paid!) or losses when panic sets in. Then the professionals buy back in again at low prices.

Even if you are a successful trader, you still need a large amount of money to play the markets cost-effectively. If you're buying and selling in millions, dealing commissions are relatively small (a half per cent per trade or so). If you trade a few thousand shares, expect to pay one and a half per cent per trade. Trade a few hundred pounds and you might pay ten per cent!

Can you hire a professional, like a stockbroker? The more money you have to invest the warmer you'll be welcomed. If you only have a few thousand pounds, you're unlikely to get a properly spread portfolio. Cynics might also suggest that it's probably not worth the broker's time advising you unless he 'churns' your stocks (buys and sells frequently to generate dealing commission) to increase his income.

There is also the paperwork. With equities, paper is generated each time you buy, sell or collect a dividend. Each company will also write to you with reports. When they want more money you'll have to sort out 'rights' issues (as a shareholder you have first refusal on new shares created by the company). Shares and gilts are relatively easy. Ever tried trading in office blocks? Being unable to invest in, say, commercial property eliminates an opportunity to achieve a more balanced, well-spread portfolio, so how does a small investor invest safely in a spread of markets?

COLLECTIVE INVESTMENTS

People with modest means can combine to spread risks, hire professionals and reduce dealing costs. Collective investments offer asset-based growth, minimal paperwork and reasonable costs without excessive risk. These are the way forward unless you are an expert in a field which gives you an edge on the big players, or you just like the fun of playing markets. But then, are you a steward for God's benefit or your gratification?

There are a variety of collective investments available which allow small savers to benefit from access to various capital markets. In all cases, though, the investor must be aware that reward tends to be proportionate to risk.

Investment trusts

These are stock exchange quoted companies who own equities to generate returns for their own shareholders. They pay dividends like any other company, and their market price reflects their popularity with investors as well as the actual value of the assets the trust owns. They may invest in a wide range of shares, or concentrate on a specific sector, like mining shares, for instance. There are a number of different types of securities issued by investment trusts, including a number which pay interest at various times. In addition, warrants confer the right to buy shares in the future. Although the specifics of these securities are beyond the scope of this book, they can have some useful and interesting applications when used by skilled professional advisors.

Unit trusts

These are funds which invest in selected sectors of the stock market. Like investment trusts, there are 'general' trusts which own a wide spectrum of shares and employ a number of specialists. Most lean towards providing either capital growth or income to the investor. Although they are mainly designed for lump sums, most good unit trust firms operate savings plans, so they are also available to small savers.

These savings plans are flexible, provide potentially good returns at a reasonable cost without excessive risk and can be stopped, started or encashed without extra cost. Whether you are investing lump sums or making regular savings these are medium-term rather than immediate access investments.

The price fluctuations of underlying assets mean unit prices rise and fall, but with good management rises should exceed falls. It is sensible to plan that the investment will not have broken even or be showing a realistic profit for a couple of years at least.

Each investment buys units in the fund at an 'offer price'. A management charge, perhaps one or two per cent of fund value, is deducted periodically, and the value of a holding is calculated by multiplying the number of units by the bid price. The bid price is the encashment value of units and is usually five to seven per cent lower than the offer price. The difference, called the Bid/Offer Spread (BOS), represents the company's up-front charges. Prices are published daily in the *Financial Times* and most 'serious' national newspapers.

We mentioned in chapter 7 that some insurance policies are also savings plans. Term policies that we met earlier are all cover with no savings. Now we can look at plans which contain an element of life assurance. Whole of life policies are mainly protection plans which run until death. Because of the policy costs they should only be used for savings under special circumstances, like certain tax planning exercises. Endowments are savings plans with just enough life cover to qualify for a tax-free payout. When considering a life assurance savings plan, pay attention to the sum assured (should be as low as possible unless you need the cover) and the term (you pay more for longer terms). Always ask whether something like a unit-trust plan is better value.

With-profit life assurance

While insurance companies waited for policyholders to die and claim benefits they invested the money to increase their income. To attract more policyholders they started to offer life assurance policies, called endowments, giving a 'sum assured' to policyholders that survived the full term. These are non-profit endowments. Monthly premium policies like these are rare today, although the lump sum type, guaranteed interest rate bonds, are quite common. Other plans also added bonuses, calculated annually to reflect the assurance

TABLE 10.1 INVESTMENT SURPLUS

This table should be used in conjunction with Table 7.3

EXISTING SAVINGS ARRANGEMENTS
Cash savings including bank, building society accounts, etc

Institution	Account no	Access period	Present balance

Asset-based savings: Life assurance, unit/investment trusts, pension plans

Institution	Plan no	Plan type	Regular payments

Value now	Maturity date	Expected value

Capital investments

Institution	Account no	Investment type	Initial value

Present value

Money available for investment £   per week/month

Capital available for investment now £

Investment goals: What will you need cash for and when?

Short term:

Medium term:

Long term:

company's profits and added to the sum assured. These are with-profit plans.

Unit-linked life assurance

These do a similar job to with-profit policies. In unit-linked plans, however, part of the premium goes to pay for life cover, part towards the company's operating costs. The rest buys units in funds run by the company. The unit price rises or falls in line with the fund's asset values and if the company does its job properly you should have a growing number of units, all increasing in value. The charging structure on the fund is similar to that for a unit trust. In addition there will probably be initial policy charges in early years to pay for marketing costs and introductory commissions. These commissions may also have a bearing on the quality of advice you receive from an advisor.

Life policies have some good features:

1. Being asset-based they tend to out-perform inflation. Policies with good companies show a long-term growth rate well above that achieved by cash saving.

2. The investment spread in with-profit policies and unit-linked managed funds includes a range of equities, cash, gilts and properties. This means that the level of risk is often lower than a unit or investment trust, but the rewards may be too.

3. There is scope for adventurous people to use specialized funds.

4. The with-profit bonus system means that the company smooths out market fluctuations, allowing steadier growth in with-profit policies.

5. They can be started for very low contribution rates, which means almost anyone can afford them.

6. The money is tax free on maturity after ten years, allowing some legitimate tax planning opportunities.

7. There is considerable legal protection for policyholders' money in the unlikely event that a company goes bust.

There are some drawbacks though:

1. You are paying for life cover which you may not need.

2. The extra charges to pay for marketing costs are taken in the early years, so it may be several years before the policy makes you a profit, especially with long-term policies. Insurance company salesmen tend to be paid in proportion to length of term and amount of life cover. Unscrupulous salesmen may write the policies over longer terms or with higher life cover to maximize their commission.

3. If you need the money back early, life company actuaries, who work out the surrender value, aren't traditionally generous.

Life policies are still good value for money if you need predictable growth over a long term and can wait for the rewards of the saving. They can be a little expensive and a bit inflexible. Those issued before 1984 receive Life Assurance Premium Relief (LAPR), which means they are partly tax deductible, with the government subsidizing the cost by half the basic rate of income tax. Policies with LAPR still attached are probably well worth keeping. (Was yours issued prior to April 1984?)

Pension plans

The subject of retirement planning is covered in greater detail elsewhere. Imagine providing your present income for maybe twenty years and you will understand why a pension is the largest investment most people ever make. The later you leave starting to plan, the more expensive it becomes, so you should make provision as early as possible. It is a long-term goal that should be part of everyone's planning, even if you only make a positive decision that you'll rely on everyone else to look after you in your old age.

If your employer isn't providing anything the pensions industry provide a wide range of pension plans. They work in the same way as life endowments or unit trust savings plans, except that all contributions you make are income tax deductible and the funds themselves pay no tax while they grow. Similar criteria will therefore apply to selecting such plans.

What are the relative merits of the various media? Let us consider two frequent queries raised by small investors.

Unit-linked or with-profit?

With-profit policies guarantee that once bonuses are added they are guaranteed. Since the insurance company cannot take the same degree of risk with the money that underlies that guarantee, it will be placed in much safer, lower yielding investments. Unit-linked policies don't make such promises and the fund can be invested more adventurously. Greater risks tend to mean greater rewards and losses, so unit-linked policies tend to be more volatile. The charges for unit-linked policies are declared more openly and so tend to be more reasonable.

Where more predictable returns are necessary, for repaying a mortgage, for example, there is a case for using a with-profit endowment. Unit-linked policies tend to be better where you need maximum long-term growth and can risk the extra volatility.

Unit/investment trusts or assurance savings plans?

The advantages of unit/investment trust savings plans are that they usually make lower initial charges and contain no penalties for changing or ceasing the plan. This allows profits to accumulate faster and be accessible quicker. They are more equity-orientated which means, on past performance, they can grow quicker but are more volatile than life assurance plans which tend to be backed by gilts and property as well as equities. Life plans are advantageous if a lower risk is required. In addition, life cover built into such plans can have some useful applications, especially in tax planning.

These are the most common collective investments for storing surplus income and building up capital. Most of them are perfectly good homes for capital itself and similar principles apply to selecting the investments.

The following alternative homes for capital are too complicated for detailed discussion in this book. A considerable amount of expertise may be required to invest safely in these areas.

Futures and commodities

Commodities are items like coffee, oil, meat, metals etc. They are closely related to futures because of the risk a producer or shipper undertakes. A ship's cargo of coffee may be bought at a certain price, but while it is at sea (often for weeks) the price may change and the shipper may find the cargo worthless when it arrives. To protect himself he sells the shipment (before he even loads it) for future delivery at a price he can accept. A speculator may feel that price can be bettered and takes on the futures contract, hoping he can sell the load for even more. If he's right he wins, if not he loses. He is taking a high risk for potentially high returns and providing an essential insurance to the coffee shipper who cannot afford such a high risk.

This principle can be used on practically anything, including minerals, currencies and foods. If a commodity can change price in the future, there is an opportunity to invite speculators to provide insurance against that change. There is a vast amount of money to be made and lost, so take care and be prepared to stand huge losses if deals go bad. There are lots of sharks after the gullible small saver, so unless you can play high-stakes poker well, it's probably best to stay away.

Options and traded options

These are a variation on futures which use price changes in quoted equities. There are courses available if you want to learn how to use options as part of your equity trading. Contact the International Stock Exchange in London.

Art, antiques, vintage cars, etc

Some spectacular opportunities exist here if you can figure out what might be fashionable in the future. The best suggestion is to also buy what you like, just in case the market doesn't agree with you.

Wine

It is only really worth investing in quality wines, and the best developed market is in fine clarets (red Bordeaux wines).

'I don't care how it's spelt. It sounds like money to me.'

The wine lives in a Bonded Warehouse (officially outside UK customs so no VAT is payable) and probably won't move unless it's delivered for drinking. You usually buy ownership through a broker. When you want to sell, the broker arranges to auction the wine and another name goes on the cases at the warehouse. Growth in its value relies on the fact that more people want to drink good claret than the French can legally make. The 'Bordeaux Index' even out-performed the Financial Times Stock Exchange Index (FT-SE) in the mid-1980s. Fine claret is deemed to be a wasting asset by the Inland Revenue so there's no Capital Gains Tax to pay either! Portfolios start at a few thousand pounds. Of course, you can always pay the VAT and have a case or two delivered if you like drinking exceptional wine which costs hundreds of pounds a bottle.

Stamps

These historically performed very well when inflation was roaring and the stock market was in the doldrums.

Gold

This tends to be the world's last resort in troubled times. Wars and other financial disasters tend to prompt a flood into gold, so the market can be a bit volatile.

Chapter Eleven

KEEPING YOUR AFFAIRS IN ORDER

Mary Bryce sat at Neil's desk and looked around the study. The week since his funeral had shot past. She had been very grateful to her in-laws for letting her and the children stay with them while they recovered from the initial shock of Neil's death, but now she had to face reality. The world was still turning and Neil would want her to get back on her feet and carry on. Mary picked up the solicitor's list again and pulled open Neil's top drawer. It had been hard enough finding all the bank statements and she couldn't imagine why the building society passbooks were kept in a different file. Now where on earth was his will . . . ?

HOW ORGANIZED ARE YOU?

Just after the Second World War, according to some older life assurance salesmen, people took death seriously. Nowadays, it seems, that people no longer talk about 'when'. Most people will talk about 'if'. Of course we all know that immortality is a myth: death is still the one guarantee in life. Yet in modern Britain it has become a taboo subject. It is not discussed in polite society and the bereaved are often shunned. Although we all accept death, intellectually at any rate, do we act as if we do?

Try this simple test. Without warning, tell your partner or the member of your family who would have to act on your death that you are dead, and ask him or her to find the following:

1. The bank and building society cheque and pass books.

2. Details, balances and the recent statements from all the accounts.

3. Your will.

4. The household and life insurance policy documents (the originals).

5. Your pension scheme documentation.

6. Details of any other investments, including the certificates.

7. The names and numbers of all your professional advisors.

If they can find them all without difficulty then congratulate yourselves. If they don't know or cannot find them, then their grief at your death may only be their first traumatic experience. You may also have left an administrative, and possibly legal, nightmare for them to suffer.

The most vital thing of all is your will. If you don't leave one, your hiding the building society account book will be the smallest problem. This chapter will start by looking at wills and their importance. Following that will be a guide to keeping everything orderly.

When someone dies leaving a valid will an executor is appointed who applies for 'probate' (the acceptance of the terms of the will by the legal authorities whose task is to ensure its terms are lawful). If you die intestate (leaving no will) the estate will be sorted out by an administrator according to the laws of intestacy. In effect your estate will be divided up according to a will written by the state. There is no guarantee that it will conform to what you would have liked if you had made a will, and every likelihood it won't. In England, for example, your parents, siblings and in-laws may all be entitled to various shares of the estate. If you were married and your estate is worth enough they could force your surviving widow(er) to sell the family home to get their share. There are in-laws who dislike their childrens' spouses enough to do it, too. If you have children your spouse may even be forced to sell the house to pay their share. Granted there is provision to get a court to overrule the intestacy laws under the Inheritance (Provision for Family and Dependants) Act 1975, but do you want your widow(er) to have to go to court to keep the home from being sold?

'. . . I wouldn't normally — but I need to ask him where he left his will.'

MAKING YOUR WILL KNOWN

Making a will is easy and cheap. The conventional advice is to see a solicitor. There are also some will writing services, but do satisfy yourself that the firm is competent to write a will. Tell the will writer what you would like to happen after you die and he will be able to write the will in a legally acceptable form. Mirror wills, in which couples leave their estates to each other, are often done at a discount, so it pays to use the same firm. You will have to nominate an executor and this should be someone you trust who should be warned in advance, since he can refuse to act. Your bank will be delighted to charge you for the service if all else fails!

You can actually make a will yourself. Lawyers would say its very unwise (but then lawyers always advise you to pay a lawyer!). Certainly you cannot afford to do it incorrectly because of the legal problems mistakes will probably create. The research needed and the care you would have to take means it probably will be cost-effective to hire a professional, especially if you have a complicated estate involving several beneficiaries or a variety of assets. Professional financial advisors should also be involved, because inheritance tax will effect all but the smallest estates. Good advice here will more than pay for the will in the long run.

When organizing your affairs, bear one other thing in mind. Probate is not granted automatically. Until it is, all assets are frozen, except for those held in joint names. It can take several months and lawyers don't always link need with speed. Your widow(er) and children won't thank you if they can't buy food for six months because you couldn't be bothered to organize things properly! To avoid problems before probate consider the following:

1. Make sure life assurance policies are written under trusts. This means that the cash misses your estate and goes straight to the intended beneficiaries. There can be tax benefits here too.

2. Make sure the company pension scheme trustees (if you're in one) have received an up-to-date 'expression

of wish' form. This tells them how you want the benefits paid out.

3. Organize bank and building society accounts so that your spouse can get to enough money to live comfortably while probate is granted.

To reduce probate delays still further and help your survivors execute your wishes, make sure that your affairs are in order. The remainder of the chapter is a personal estate organizer, which you should complete.

PERSONAL ESTATE ORGANIZER

IN THE EVENT OF MY DEATH PLEASE NOTIFY
1. Name   Relationship
Address & telephone

2. Name   Relationship
Address & telephone

MY WILL:
     Was made on   /   /   and last reviewed on   /   /
     Codicil attached on   /   /
     Kept at:

DESIRED FUNERAL ARRANGEMENTS

KEY DOCUMENTS KEPT AT:
Birth certificate:
Marriage certificate:
Other certificates:
Insurance policies:
Life assurance policies:
Pension scheme documents:
Property/mortgage deeds:
Bank and building society passbooks:
Bank and building society account details:
List of investments:
Share, unit trust certificates, etc:
Tax records:
Car documents:
Donor cards:
Keys:
Other key documents:

MY EXECUTORS ARE
Name   Relationship
Address and telephone

Name   Relationship
Address and telephone

LIFE ASSURANCE ARRANGEMENTS
Assurance company and claims address

Policy number   Policy type
Policy commenced on   /   /   and will expire/mature on   /   /
Sum assured £   Guaranteed minimum death benefit £
Policy assigned to (if applicable):

Assurance company and claims address

Policy number   Policy type
Policy commenced on   /   /   and will expire/mature on   /   /
Sum assured £   Guaranteed minimum death benefit £
Policy assigned to (if applicable):

Assurance company and claims address

Policy number   Policy type
Policy commenced on   /   /   and will expire/mature on   /   /
Sum assured £   Guaranteed minimum death benefit £
Policy assigned to (if applicable):

Assurance company and claims address

Policy number   Policy type
Policy commenced on   /   /   and will expire/mature on   /   /
Sum assured £   Guaranteed minimum death benefit £
Policy assigned to (if applicable):

PENSION ARRANGEMENTS
Company scheme & address

Basis of pension entitlement

Amount of benefit at last review

Death-in-service benefit (if any) £

Beneficiaries nominated on 'expression of wish' form:
Name   Relationship
Address and telephone

Name   Relationship
Address and telephone

FREE STANDING ADDITIONAL VOLUNTARY CONTRIBUTIONS, PERSONAL & SELF EMPLOYED PENSIONS
1. Pension provider and address

Policy number   Policy type (PP or s226)
Commenced on   /   /   to select retirement date   /   /
Premium presently is £   per annum/month.
Fund at last review £

2. Pension provider and address

Policy number   Policy type (PP or s226)
Commenced on   /   /   to select retirement date   /   /
Premium presently is £   per annum/month
Fund at last review £

3. Pension provider and address

Policy number   Policy type (PP or s226)
Commenced on   /   /   to select retirement date   /   /
Premium presently is £   per annum/month
Fund at last review £

4. Pension provider and address

Policy number   Policy type (PP or s226)
Commenced on   /   /   to select retirement date   /   /
Premium presently is £   per annum/month
Fund at last review £

5. Pension provider and address

Policy number   Policy type (PP or s226)
Commenced on   /   /   to select retirement date   /   /
Premium presently is £   per annum/month
Fund at last review £

PERMANENT HEALTH INSURANCE
Insurer and address

Policy number
Benefit and frequency
Deferment period
Policy commenced on   /   /   and expires on   /   /

PERSONAL ACCIDENT COVER
Insurer and address

Policy number
Cover

OTHER INSURANCES
Insurer
Address
Cover type
Policy number

Insurer
Address
Cover type
Policy number

Insurer
Address
Cover type
Policy number

FINANCIAL OBLIGATIONS CEASING ON DEATH
Include nature of obligation and reason why it ceases on death.

CONTINUING FINANCIAL OBLIGATIONS
Eg commitments to dependents, other relatives, loan guarantees

RESPONSIBILITIES
Eg director, club official, charity organizer, employee, regular visitor

OUTSTANDING LEGAL MATTERS
Advisors:
Insurance broker
Address
Contact and telephone:

Independent Financial Advisor
Address
Contact and telephone:

Accountant
Address
Contact and telephone:

Solicitor
Address
Contact and telephone:

Stockbroker
Address
Contact and telephone:

Other
Address
Contact and telephone:

ASSETS

1. Bank/building society

Telephone and contact
Sort Code: /   /
Account numbers and type
Account name(s) and signatory

2. Bank/building society

Telephone and contact
Sort code: /   /
Account numbers and type
Account name(s) and signatory

3. Bank/building society

Telephone and contact
Sort code: /   /
Account numbers and type
Account name(s) and signatory

4. Bank/building society

Telephone and contact
Sort code: /   /
Account numbers and type
Account name(s) and signatory

CREDIT CARDS

Company

Number

Expiry date

CHEQUE CARDS
Bank/Building Society   Number   Expiry date

MAIN RESIDENCE
Address

Joint owners
Freehold/leasehold   Ground landlord

Local authority

Insured value   Insurer & policy number

Contents value

Mortgage lender and address

          Account number

OTHER PRIORITIES

OTHER ASSETS
Include description, approximate value and location. Lists of
individual securities such as equities, unit trusts etc, should be
kept separately and the list's location recorded under 'Other
key documents'.

MEDICAL
Doctor, name, address and telephone

NHS number

Private medical insurer and address

Policy number and cover

OTHER INFORMATION
Tax district address and telephone

Tax ref no:

National Insurance number

AA/RAC   Membership number
Cover   Renewal   /   /

Other memberships
Include organization, address, member number, contacts etc.

NOTES

Chapter Twelve

THINKING BIG, THINKING DANGEROUSLY

My Lord Bishop

I am writing to protest at the activities at St Allsbright's, Buttemuddled-in-the-Weye. I am but one parishoner disturbed at the way church life has been all but ruined in recent years by the Reverend Robert Ward and his new ideas.

We are the long-standing members of a church now full of hundreds of malcontents. We may be the minority but only against outsiders, many with nothing more than a dubious desire to 'meet Jesus', whatever that means. What are still referred to as Sunday Services are now so loud one cannot hear oneself think during the hymns.

Were this a purely religious matter I would move to a different church. There are, however, various subversives at work whom a number of us find disturbing. I have chosen to stay and try to preserve the real fabric of English life in our church.

We were all in agreement with Ward's plan for bulk purchases of groceries throughout the town on a co-operative basis. My colleagues and I supplied goods at generous discounts. Those needing them, especially housebound elderly people, enjoyed home-delivered groceries at better than supermarket prices. As local traders we were pleased to help. My wife and I even noticed that Sunday shoppers were saved the trouble and the local superstore even ceased Sunday trading due to lack of demand.

We did not envisage the latest developments in the church's activities. Not content with his alternative to Sunday trading, Ward's team now supply free food and groceries to scroungers in supposed need. A local block of flats now forms a hostel – full, needless to say – of all kinds of ne'er-do-wells, even parolled prisoners and homeless addicts. Walking the streets isn't safe in a formerly picturesque part of the county. Next he plans to bring parties of slum children to the town for 'evangelistic' holidays. These foolhardy schemes are, needless to say, financed by the church plate to which I am a regular contributor.

The physical threat to our citizens is matched only by the likely decline in property values. Many here have achieved security after years of hard work. We all agree that something must be done to solve the problems these people face but it is inappropriate for the church to meddle in commerce. The naive approach that Reverend Ward and his well-meaning but misguided team are taking can only end in disaster.

Finally, we are disturbed by the 'Third World Network' that is growing through this and, I gather from political colleagues, many churches Europewide. The church selling cheap coffee to my customers I can tolerate, but the range of goods is growing, supplied on terms that a real business cannot hope to match. Furthermore the political pressure this network now exerts on the Government may even lead to loss of Anglican privileges in consequence. On a local level I feel that dividing the not insignificant profits amongst network members not used to wealth is highly dangerous.

My Lord, this man undermines the traditional fabric of our religion and may even threaten our national way of life. I would be grateful if you can rid us of this troublesome cleric before he bankrupts us all.

Your sincerely
Arthur Silverspoon
Major (retd.) Chairman, Silverspoon Investments plc.

The Bishop parked his car by Church House, the small office block which St Allsbright had leased opposite the churchyard. Most churches preserved the same appearance and atmosphere at every visit, one or two were even locked in a time warp. When he visited Robert, on the other hand, which was every six months on average, he was never quite sure how the place would look or what he would find. A more traditional bishop could well be unsettled by the constant change. A modern office block? he wondered. But then where else would one set up a modern office, especially if you had the money to expand beyond the role of unpaid keeper of Britain's architectural heritage?

And St Allsbright had money. It paid so much 'quota' to the diocese it embarrassed some clergy whose churches had to run fetes and bazaars to raise their salaries, especially when, for the last year or so at least, St Allsbright had often paid towards those stipends too. Eyebrows weren't so much raised as frozen wide in disbelief. Yet the Archdeacon's annual visitation, for which he was now accompanied by an accountant, so extensive were the books, had never raised a murmur of a problem.

The church had started with a Credit Union to pool money for small, low-interest rate loans to members. That vision now included a community bank providing starter loans and financial support for local businesses. The church and its contacts provided a ready market for many of them, which helped the survival rate, and the profits cycled back to the bank, the church members who invested in it and, through tithing, to the church itself.

One of its first in-house investments had been a community grocery co-operative which provided its members with home-delivered groceries, now at nearly wholesale prices. The church then joined a shopping club, distributing goods from the Third World, and set up a snack bar. This had all been achieved in the teeth of opponents who objected to the church straying from generally accepted 'religious interests'. They had a point. It was getting harder to see the division between spiritual and secular activities, but then which bit of life does the Bible say God isn't interested in?

The profits from the operations were growing so quickly that a Mission Council with two full-time employees was needed just to filter the requests for money and monitor the church's participation in those projects which it decided to support. Other churches in the town, from a variety of denominations, had joined in and now jointly operated many of the projects. The hostel for homeless people, child-minding groups and daughter churches in various parts of the town were among the works that served the demand from Buttemuddled-in-the-Weye.

These latter caused bitterness amongst, mainly Anglican, clergy. They were horrified at some of the projects anyway, then very angry when residents for whom they felt they had 'cure of souls' first joined St Allsbright, then set up regular fellowships in their parish territories. Wasn't this poaching, they cried, when there was plenty of space in their own empty churches? Beyond the town there were church-twinning and missionary projects in Britain and abroad. This one little parish in a small town in England had, in a few years, built an international fellowship that matched the electoral roll of the whole of the rest of the diocese put together. And since St Allsbright had as many non-members in various parts of its fellowship, the Bishop reckoned you could double it again.

The double doors to the foyer of the offices were open. The Honesty snack bar to the left was doing a rapid trade that lunch-time and Linda Saunders, Robert's PA, was hovering with one eye on a packed seminar room to the right where about forty people were watching a video. As the bishop walked in her face lit up and she crossed to him, gave him a big hug and kissed both his cheeks.

'Bishop Joshua! Great to see you again. Robert asked me to meet you as he's going to be tied up for a few minutes with the seminar. It's his turn to do the closing address. I gather you said he wasn't to re-arrange his diary so I have the pleasure of entertaining you at the snack bar.'

She led him across the foyer and sat him down in a corner table while she collected some coffee. He was able to acknowledge the waved greetings from a couple of St Allsbright regulars busy in discussions over their lunch.

'Hello, Steve,' said the bishop to Steve Storey, noting the sun-tanned face, 'been on holiday?'

'Sort of,' Steve replied. 'Training attachment to a twin church in Botswana. They're growing at a fantastic pace over there and lack enough trained leaders. We go over with teaching aids and money, and help train their pastors.'

'Sounds like valuable work'

'Immensely. I've learned so much about real Christian living. They may be materially poor but they have so much spiritual riches. I reckon that's why they're growing so fast. Makes you see how wealth can blind you to real faith if you're not careful. From their point of view it's more cost effective too. They used two of us to train thirty of their people. Imagine how much it would have cost to fly thirty of them to theological college here?'

'Would our theological colleges have been culturally relevant to their needs, do you think?' asked the bishop, 'I've not been to Botswana.'

'Can't really say, all my theological training was by extension study. I guess it would be an interesting factor to consider.'

Linda returned from the bar. He had mentioned an Honesty bar to his cathedral staff after a previous visit and met blank looks and disbelief. The idea had appealed to him when he noticed the sign over the counter which read:

THE PRICES QUOTED ARE COST PRICE AND RETAIL PRICE ASSUMING A 15% MARGIN. PLEASE PAY AT THE COUNTER. IF YOU CANNOT AFFORD OUR FULL PRICES PLEASE PAY WHAT YOU CAN. IF YOU ARE WEALTHY PLEASE PAY EXTRA TO COVER THOSE WHO CAN PAY NOTHING. THE COLLECTION POINT NEAR THE EXIT IS FOR EITHER PURPOSE.

Mr and Mrs Pomfrey, who had set up and run the bar since Mr Pomfrey's retirement from his job as a bank manager, followed Linda over.

'How's business, Mr P?' asked the bishop.

'Revelational,' Pomfrey replied. 'We've been open to the

public for about a year on the honesty basis.' The bishop knew that the bar had started life as an honesty bar in the church kitchen for the staff. The staff had increased, then the church members started to use it. Eventually the word spread and Mr Pomfrey, bored with golf and gardening six days a week, had suggested setting it up as a proper business. 'Even when overheads are taken into account we're doing fine.' Mrs Pomfrey's home cooking and her husband's custom-built sandwiches had been credited in the local paper with decimating the profits at the town's fast-food shops.

'I know the food and the prices are attractive,' said the bishop, 'but don't people abuse the system?'

'Occasionally, of course. But you get to know the real needy people, though you respect people's privacy if they do need a free meal. In any case they're more than covered by the extra donations people give, because the townspeople feel it's their facility. The abusers tend to be identifiable after a few visits and we just send in a pastoral visitor.'

'Why not the police?' asked the bishop.

'If they're ripping off a place like this,' explained Mrs Pomfrey, 'they must be sad people who really need Jesus. Or they may have genuine financial problems. We arrange for a councillor to sit with them next time they're in. They're either glad to have an offer of help or they vanish so fast at the name of Jesus,' she started to laugh, 'that they're never seen again. But actually, Bishop, most people are honest when you assume the best of them and expect it of them. Linda here is too young, but I remember a time when you didn't need to lock up your house because hardly anyone would break in.'

'The local traders surely object, don't they?'

'Instinctively, yes,' said Mr Pomfrey, 'They thought we'd send them under first, then go under ourselves and leave them with no livelihood and the town with no restaurants. But most of them know me and my track record. They realise we're serious about meeting genuine public demand and that we're here for good. Whenever a trader's in trouble I go to see whether we can provide him with some business. Not all our food is prepared here, for instance. If there is something we need, we'd rather use a local business. By and large we're accepted now. The VAT people were the biggest problem.'

'VAT is difficult, is it?' asked the bishop.

'It's surprising how an essentially simple tax can be made so complicated to administer. The books aren't a problem, it was just persuading them we were a business and intending to be profitable. They didn't see how we could do it and give away free food, although our VAT returns have convinced them. We have some of their inspectors eating here quite regularly,

'It felt more appropriate than a graph.'

though we're not sure if they like the food or if they're just trying to figure us out.'

'Do they pay?'

'But of course. Nice to find honest tax collectors, isn't it?' he smiled. 'Bishop, nice to see you. Please excuse us, enjoy your coffee, and we've a spot of lunch ready for when you and Robert want it. Don't forget to pay when you leave.'

The bishop laughed. 'God bless you and I'd like you to talk to the staff at my cathedral about opening there, although I gather the cathedral's intention is to milk the tourists to pay for the maintenance, which might not be compatible with your vision here.'

'Call me, we'll talk,' replied Mr Pomfrey as he and his wife disappeared into the kitchen.

Linda was sitting opposite the bishop. He savoured the coffee, then asked, 'How is young David progressing?'

'Oh, he's fine. We started him at junior school this term and he loves it. Still, he's got all his friends with him which must help. With all the churches in the town there are enough pre-school kids to fill the creche and baby-minding facilities, so the children tend to be together in the creche, then on to the local nursery and so on.'

'Lots of parents use the service?'

'Oh yes. Peter and I both have to work.' She smiled at him conspiratorially. 'You remember the little hiccup we had when he was born. Well, we've expanded the original creche system for those working in the church to include an all-day baby-minding service and a pre-nursery school playgroup. It means that church members who commute can leave their children safely, with proper facilities and qualified staff. We've even persuaded the PCC to subsidize the costs.'

'Church members only?'

'Who's a member of the church and who isn't? Originally it was set up for the church members and workers but – since you were last here actually anyone "in the community" can join. We've had to put a flexible geographical limit on it, so we can control numbers without excluding deserving people who happen to live ten yards over the parish line or something stupid. After all, the community will get the kids it deserves regardless of faith, so a bit of common sense is needed, isn't it?'

'Don't people accuse you of encouraging mothers to leave their children and work?'

'Not to my knowledge,' Linda bristled, 'and in any case, how are single parents supposed to feed their kids if they don't work. Not everyone can afford to be an unwaged parent, you know!'

Robert Ward arrived and tapped the bishop on the shoulder. Mrs Pomfrey, back behind the counter, caught his eye and got an affirmative to another round of coffees.

'Sorry, Joshua. I was on the rota to do a seminar.'

'Don't worry. As I explained on the phone, this isn't formal and it gave me the chance to get an update on the nursery and the snack bar. They seem to be doing excellent work.'

'They certainly are,' replied Robert, as Linda finished her coffee, excused herself, and linked up with one of the young men leaving the seminar looking thoughtful. 'After all the teething problems we've come through, praise the Lord.'

'Praise him indeed,' agreed the bishop. 'What was the seminar for? It seemed very well attended.'

'Network Christianity,' declared Robert, 'our latest venture.'

'Dare I ask what "Network Christianity" is? Am I likely to receive yet more complaints about my most "troublesome cleric"?'

'You never know your luck,' grinned Robert in reply. 'It's a simple idea, based on Acts 8. As you know, the church has always expanded fastest when Christians talk to non-Christians about Jesus. Trouble is, though, hardly anyone knows how to explain Christianity to another soul. Makes you wonder how Paul was so successful with the Gentiles, doesn't it? Then one of the clergy most opposed to the Third World Network said, rather crossly: "If all your Network were as keen on spreading the word as you are on making money, I'd be more convinced." Good point, I thought, especially since the biggest problem we have with our network is that some of our people are tempted to abuse some quite serious earnings from it.

'Then one of the network trainers pointed out that the greatest network sales opportunity was salvation through Jesus. Why didn't we apply the network marketing techniques we use to move goods from the Third World to tell the people about Jesus? So we had a tape made. People only need to be able to operate "Play" on a video and it gives a fifteen-minute message which ends up inviting them to a local meeting. That was the meeting you saw a few minutes ago.

'At the meeting we preach a bit more of the gospel. Those interested go to an Enquirer's Group where they can discuss their own questions. If and when they're ready they can join the church proper, make a commitment and be baptized. Throughout the process they're encouraged to bring their friends, family, anyone else.'

'Are you having a good response?'

'Like selling water in a desert. We've sold 600 tapes in four weeks. We're entertaining forty people a meeting, twice daily. We've doubled the Enquirer Groups already and have a waiting list as soon as we can train leaders. We haven't yet launched meetings in our daughter churches because we can't yet cope with the demand from the new enquirers.'

'What's the secret?' asked the Bishop.

'The Holy Spirit and the word of God. All we've done is package it to take advantage of modern technology. Anyone who can load a video can tell his friends about the gospel. As you've always said, the Word is like a "smart" missile. As God's soldiers we just launch it. The Holy Spirit guides it to its target and controls the result.

'We train everyone to show the video and say: "I think this

is brilliant, do you see anything in it for you?" Funnily enough people do, quite often. We've even had enquirers come back with friends just to see the gospel, even though they haven't yet made their own minds up. The Pentecostals would never believe what's been happening in a fuddy-duddy Anglican church!'

'May I take a video to watch myself?'

'Sure, but we sent one to the diocese a few weeks ago. Did someone pinch it?'

'Doubt it,' the bishop replied. 'Knowing my staff, someone filed it. Keep me informed, especially if you need trained Enquirer Group leaders. I'm sure we can get some willing volunteers to work with one of famous St Allsbright teams.'

'Or infamous, to judge from the letter you told me about. Who was it from?'

'Unless I think there are grounds for formal action there's little point in telling you, is there?'

'I suppose not,' agreed Robert glumly. 'It would be nice to know where the poisoned pens are, that's all.'

'You mean you don't know already?' asked the bishop in a disbelieving tone.

'I suppose I can guess. What's he complaining about now?'

'The Third World Network and it's threat to "real", by which I presume he means his own, business and to the Anglican church if the network embarrasses the Prime Minister, who might be tempted to take retaliatory action. He says the hostel's effect on local property is devastating, the streets aren't safe and too many poor people are getting too much money all at his expense as a church plate contributor. Those are the bullet points anyway.'

'I can guess who one of his "too many poor people . . ." is. Mike, our network leader, joined the Major's golf club . . . Oh sorry. I wasn't supposed to know who wrote the letter, was I? Mike Jones is an ex-prisoner who found Jesus through the hostel scheme and has made a good living through the network by recruiting new members throughout the town. He's bought a house locally and now plays golf. Since half the PCC are also on the Golf Club Committee he didn't find much trouble getting a membership. Your "correspondent" must be really upset now that, having found his church full of the wrong sort of people, they're now joining his Golf Club.'

'What about this political side, then? My correspondent claims political inside knowledge of danger to the Anglican Church.'

'The point about the Third World Network, as you know, was to find help for people from countries who needed access to our markets but couldn't get it without our help. Network marketing was used because it's the most cost-effective way of generating that market penetration since it grows on word-of-mouth referrals. Why do you think Jesus uses it to spread the gospel? It also means the distribution system is owned by the customers, which means they get profits – Mike's income, for example, along with the suppliers in the Third World. It's a sort of co-operative really.

'In fact, it's worked so well in the three years from launch that we've begun to hit problems with EC legislation. We can't import some goods from the Third World at the prices our suppliers can sell at because of restrictive trade practices. And if that wasn't bad enough, remember the EC dumps millions of tons of food in the Third World to stop us buying cheaper food here. That means local farmers and businesses can't make a living selling at home because they can't compete with artificially low-priced goods from the EC. They can't sell to us because the EC forces their prices up here. That's perhaps an oversimplification but you get the idea, don't you? Are we surprised that millions in the Third World are dependent on aid?'

'And the Network is now putting pressure on the government to change the rules?'

'The Network is EC wide and we're now putting pressure on all the governments. Frankly I doubt if the Anglican church will be singled out. The Network has members in all religions and most political parties, EC-wide. We're hoping to do for Fair Trade policies what Body Shop did for animal experimentation.'

The bishop thought for a moment. 'The suggestion was made in the letter that my correspondent's money was being risked on your dangerous projects. I assume that's nonsense.'

'Your correspondent, assuming I've guessed right, is one of those who religiously sticks in his smallest silver coin each week. We respect a widow's mite, sure, but from a millionaire? And in any case, they're not my ideas. I just preached a series of sermons on money. My parishioners, I suspect like most congregations, contained a whole clutch of leaders, teachers, adminstrators, all sorts. They realised what God was saying to them and the ideas flooded in. The problem has been identifying the ones God want's us to do something about.

'Not all of them are financial projects, are they?' asked the bishop.

'No, but you try starting a restaraunt, or a hostel, or a community warehouse, or a church-twinning project overseas without some seed capital. Once money started coming in we re-invested to expand the work. Now the church and many of it's members are involved in the businesses which, let's face it, serve the community. If they didn't, neither the church nor the businesses would be growing so fast, would they?'

'How do you justify the church getting involved in all these projects?'

'That's the sort of question asked by people who despise the church because it's irrelevant to modern life,' said Robert, a touch bitterly, 'then get annoyed when it becomes both relevant and popular. They actually want the church to dish out irrelevant religion so that it won't challenge their lifestyle. The justification is quite simple: This is God's church, his works, his people are served, his gospel proclaimed, either by example, in the way we do business, or in so many words, like in our Sunday services or the Network videos.' Robert paused as he saw the Bishop smiling quietly at his outburst.

'You're the bishop. It's your job to oversee our work to ensure it doesn't dishonour God. You tell me where God disapproves of this.'

'That's the kind of answer I need to hear occasionally,' replied the bishop. 'Troublesome clerics like you the church needs a few more of. This place is so vibrant it reminds me of my family's church in the Caribbean.'

Dear Major Silverspoon

Thank you very much for your recent letter, one of many about various aspects of the work at St Allsbright. I keep, with my staff, a close eye, not least because approximately half the electoral roll of the diocese attend that church and its various fellowships. The situation is frequently in my mind and in my prayers.

I understand how you may feel about the changes in recent years and I support and admire your determination to stay in the church and contribute to its life in the way God leads you. May I ask you to pray and meditate with God about the church in the context of a Bible passage that may have relevance here. As a traditional Anglican I know you will have great respect for God's word.

The apostles were challenged by the religious authorities of their day (Acts 5:17–39) who demanded action to stop their proclamation of Messiah. A wise Pharisee named Gamaliel advised caution, pointing out that many others had proclaimed messiahs at that time. 'It all came to nothing,' he said. 'Therefore I advise you, leave these men alone! Let them go! For if their purpose or activity is of human origin it will fail. But if it is from God, you will not be able to stop these men; you will find yourself fighting against God.'

Please feel free to visit me and we can compare the Lord's guidance.

Yours sincerely
Joshua Marley
Bishop